CARLOS NOW THE DAWN'S NO FOND ILLUSION

THE AUTHOR

Tomás Borge was born in Matagalpa in 1930 and went to school there with Carlos Fonseca. They were fellow students at the University of León and in 1961, together with Silvio Mayorga, they founded the Sandinista National Liberation Front (FSLN). As a clandestine militant Tomás was captured in Managua on 4th February 1976 and imprisoned by the dictator's National Guard. Hooded, handcuffed and severely tortured in prison, he wrote poetry and, after hearing of the death of Carlos Fonseca on 8th November 1976, he wrote this memoir of him: *Carlos, el Amanecer ya no es una Tentación (Carlos, Now the Dawn's no Fond Illusion)*.

He was released, together with fifty-eight other political prisoners, as a result of the FSLN assault on the National Palace on 22nd August 1978, where they held the deputies to ransom for two days. This action sparked off insurrections all over the country, beginning with Matagalpa, and the following year, on July 19th 1979, the revolutionary forces entered Managua in triumph.

With the triumph of the Revolution, Tomás Borge became Minister of the Interior (Home Secretary). When he was in prison, he had promised to have revenge on his torturers, and as Minister of the Interior, his 'revenge' was to visit and forgive them.

His memoirs, *La Paciente impaciencia*, appeared from Editorial Vanguardia, Managua, in 1989 (*The Patient Impatience*: Curbstone Press, Connecticut 1992) and a collection of his poetry, *La Ceremonia Esperada,* from Editorial Nueva Nicaragua, Managua, in 1990. Some of these poems and Luis Enrique Mejía Godoy's song 'Revenge', based on Borge's words, are translated by Dinah Livingstone in *Poets of the Nicaraguan Revolution* (Katabasis 1993).

1966. FROM LEFT TO RIGHT. BACK ROW, STANDING: CARLOS FONSECA, ROBERTO AMAYA, FAUSTO AMADOR, OSCAR TURCIOS.
FRONT ROW: DANIEL ORTEGA, TOMÁS BORGE, ROLANDO ROQUE.

CARLOS,
NOW THE DAWN'S
NO FOND ILLUSION

Tomás Borge

Translated by Dinah Livingstone

KATABASIS

First published in 1996 by KATABASIS
10 St Martins Close, London NW1 0HR (0171 485 3830)
Copyright: Tomás Borge
Translation Copyright: Dinah Livingstone
Printed by Antony Rowe, Chippenham (01249 659705)
Cover printed by Aldgate Press, London (0171 247 3015)
The cover photograph shows Carlos Fonseca in La Aviación prison, Managua in 1964.
The text of *Carlos, el Amanecer ya no es una Tentación* is taken from *Nicaráuac*, 13 (Managua, December 1986).

Trade Distribution: Password Books
23 New Mount Street
Manchester M4 4DE (0161 953 4009)

ISBN: 0 904872 25 4

British Library Cataloguing in Publication Data:
A catalogue record for this book is available
from the British Library.

ACKNOWLEDGMENTS

KATABASIS and the translator would like to thank the poet Julio Valle-Castillo very much for his help and advice, and for the precious copy of *Nicararáuc* 13, containing the best available Spanish text. Special thanks to Kelly Walker and Grace Livingstone for proof reading the Spanish and English text.

KATABASIS is grateful for the support of the Arts Council of England.

LIST OF ILLUSTRATIONS

CONTENTS

CARLOS, EL AMANECER YA NO ES UNA TENTACIÓN

INTRODUCCIÓN

El que escribe estas líneas se parece tanto a un escritor, como García Márquez a un vendedor de frigoríficos. Estas líneas tienen, sin embargo, un mérito: fueron escritas casi totalmente en la cárcel, poseídas por el dios de la furia y el demonio de la ternura.

Dedico este pequeño esfuerzo a mi hermano Modesto, el jefe guerrillero más modesto, terco, fraterno y honesto que ha producido el Frente Sandinista de Liberación Nacional y a los combatientes de la montaña que viven, cantan y luchan en cada emboscada, en cada fatiga, en la orilla del sol y los sueños de Carlos Fonseca.

I

Ese estallido de poemas rimados, de aprender a bailar, de visitar la acera de enfrente bajo un farol iluminado de miradas, de incursionar en las haciendas para encontrar el secreto de la cuajada fresca y el venado al alcance del rifle .22, compartir con los amigos las delicias y las tensiones del Winitú; cuando escribíamos cartas de letras cuidadosas para descubrir en el último momento que la Vilma es la novia de Aníbal, y admirábamos a Guillermo porque tenía los ojos con magnetismo personal − no se masturbaba en pandilla − y todas las muchachas le decían adiós.

Fue la hora de Teresita, la de pecas importantes, ojos negros, dicción incorregible, de escalofríos, para susurrar tal vez; de los aniversarios a Bolívar: 'Si hay aquí algún

CARLOS, NOW THE DAWN'S NO FOND ILLUSION

INTRODUCTION

The person writing this is no more a writer than García Márquez is a refrigerator salesman. However, these lines have one merit: they were written almost entirely in prison, possessed by the god of fury and the demon of tenderness.

I dedicate this little effort to my brother Modesto,[1] the most modest, stubborn, kind and decent guerrilla leader the Sandinista National Liberation Front has ever produced, and to the mountain combatants who live, sing and struggle on together with Carlos Fonseca, through every ambush, all their exhaustion, looking forward to the same sunrise and dreaming the same dreams.

I

That outburst of rhymed poems, learning to dance, crossing to the opposite pavement under a blaze of staring eyes, expeditions to farms to discover the secret of fresh junket and deer to be shot with a .22 rifle, sharing the delights and excitements of Winitú with friends; painfully composing letters only to discover at the last minute that Vilma is Aníbal's girlfriend. We admired Guillermo because he had magnetic eyes — he did not masturbate with the gang — and all the girls called out hello to him.

It was the time of Teresita, when a spot on your face could be a disaster, black eyes, crude language, shudders, whispers, anniversaries of Bolívar: 'If anyone here is an

---

1.   Henry Ruiz.

3

enemigo de la libertad que se lo trague la tierra; está por llegar Bolívar con un látigo en la mano para sacarlo del templo.' El templo es un patio con sillas proclives a la decrepitud y a la sorpresa. Poco después *Espartaco*, semanario que se vendió como pan caliente y en el que se escribía vaga pero fervorosamente de Sandino.

Quién sabe si porque tenía los ojos negros o porque Marina cantaba en voz baja y persistente, el hecho es que así, de pronto, apareció el malestar, el escalofrío, la magia. Tal vez porque el río sonaba cerca de sus rodillas intermitentes o sólo porque era la primera muchacha con olor a noche y a sudor que me miraba a los ojos; lo cierto es que estaba triste y esquivo.

Confieso que era difícil incluso para mí, pitcher de una tribu de cipotes que recién entrenaban una nueva voz, ponerse triste. Los domingos, imposible. Por las noches sí porque leíamos a Flaubert, a Becker, y a Karl May.

Cuando nos hicimos antisomocistas, leíamos a Alberto Masferrer y nos metieron presos, dejamos de estar tristes, de ser adolescentes y de ir a las procesiones a piropear muchachas.

II

En ese instante apareció Carlos Fonseca. Llegó hasta nosotros con sus ojos bruscos, miopes y azules; contundente, serio, cordial, de pantalones blancos brincacharcos, de gestos extensos. En el Instituto: 10 en Algebra, en Francés y todo lo demás. En la calle, de largas piernas rápidas − era cartero para ayudar a doña Justina, su madre − sin detenerse a observar las miradas indeclinables que depositan en el remitente quienes reciben una carta, con

enemy of liberty, let the earth swallow him; Bolívar is about to arrive with a whip in his hand to drive him out of the temple!' The temple is a patio whose decrepit chairs might let you down suddenly. Shortly afterwards, *Spartacus*, a weekly that sold like hot cakes, in which there were vague but fervent references to Sandino.

Who knows whether it was Marina's black eyes or because she sang in a low urgent voice, the fact was that, suddenly, there was awkwardness, shivering, magic. Perhaps because a glimpse of her knees brought the sound of the river near, or just because she was the first girl smelling of night and sweat who looked into my eyes — anyway I was moody and ill at ease.

I admit it was difficult, even for me — the top baseball pitcher in a gang of youths whose voices had recently broken — to be sad. On Sundays, impossible. At night it was different, because then we read Flaubert, Becker and Karl May.

When we became anti-Somocistas, we read Alberto Masferrer and they arrested us, we stopped being sad, stopped being adolescents and going to processions to chat up girls.

II

At that moment Carlos Fonseca appeared. He came up to us with his staring, short-sighted blue eyes; forceful, serious, cordial, wearing white drainpipe trousers, gesticulating. At the Institute: 10 in Algebra, French and everything else. In the street he strode along swiftly on his long legs — he was was a postman to help Doña Justina, his mother — not stopping to observe the curious glances of those who received a letter. He carried a book under his arm to read at

un libro bajo el brazo en los entreactos. Las primeras reuniones fueron en el patio de la Lala, con sombras de pájaros, jocotes y naranjas. Descubrimos a Tomás Moro, a John Steinbeck; después, el hallazgo de Marx y Engels, localizados en la polvorosa librería del poeta Samuel Meza. Lenin fue una difícil y lejana ilusión bibliográfica inlocalizable en la oscurana.

Desde el inicio en aquellas tardes interrumpidas por jícaras de leche con pinol, Carlos dirigió, sin proponérselo, nuestros primeros esfuerzos para entender algo distinto de lo que nos decían en las aulas, en los periódicos, en las iglesias.

Un par de años atrás quería ser santo — según me dijo después en confidencias inevitables. Lo vimos hacer la primera comunión en ceremonia pálida de niños pobres y candela blanca con motivos de papel dorado, que su madre guardó en una larga caja de madera donde depositó por varios años los recuerdos cada día más sonoros e irreprochables del hijo.

Cuando ya no quería ser santo — pero seguía siéndolo de todos modos — con Chico Buitrago fundó *Segovia*, revista de símbolos extraños y editoriales premonitorios.

III

Cuando llegamos a la Universidad, lloró con esa ferocidad que a veces tiene la tristeza. Ojos azules llorando, ¿y quién no? La Universidad era un techo, algunas paredes, un corredor indiferente, obsceno, sin nostalgias conocidas y con tufillo a disección de perros abandonados: el reflujo.

intervals. Our first meetings were in Lala's patio, with its shadows of birds, hog plum and orange trees. We discovered Thomas More and John Steinbeck; later we found Marx and Engels, located in the poet Samuel Meza's dusty bookshop. Lenin was an obscure bibliographical reference not to be found in the dark.

From the beginning during those afternoons punctuated by calabash goblets of milk with *pinol*,[2] Carlos, without intending to, became the leader of our first efforts to understand something different from what we were being told in lecture rooms, newspapers and churches.

A few years earlier he had wanted to be a saint — according to what he told me later in inevitable shared secrets. We saw him making his first communion with the modest ceremony of poor children carrying the white candle decorated with gold paper. This was kept by his mother in a large wooden box where, over the years, she stored the mementoes of her son, which daily became more impressive.

When he no longer wanted to be a saint — but he continued to be one in any case — with Chico Buitrago he founded *Segovia*, a journal of strange symbols and premonitory editorials.

III

When we arrived at University, he cried with the ferocity that sadness sometimes has. Blue eyes weeping. And who did not? The University was a roof, a few walls, an indifferent, obscene corridor, without any cherished memories and stinking of dissected stray dogs: flotsam.

---

2.   Nicaraguan drink made with ground maize.

Carlos se hizo hormiga, martillo, mecanógrafo y, desde entonces, sempiterno. Repartió letreros subversivos de pared en pared, y periódicos estudiantiles y partidarios de casa en casa. Casi de inmediato se publicó *El Universitario*, de titulares gruesos y a dos colores, en el que se intercalaron sin metáforas, datos estadísticos: 250.000 niños en edad escolar sin escuelas y sin maestros (ahora son 400.000); 5% de impuestos, por el oro exportado, a las compañías mineras, e impuestos eximidos a las mismas, por maquinaria agrícola y minera, automóviles, artefactos eléctricos, etc. Números: nuestro país paga a los extranjeros que explotan el subsuelo para que se lleven el oro. Nos queda la tos.

IV

Por esa época fuimos reclutados a medias por el Partido Socialista, y Carlos dirigió la primera célula marxista de estudiantes universitarios nicaragüenses: — Silvio Mayorga era uno de los tres militantes. Un leonés que vivió en México y que nunca se supo si fue 'charro' o militante marxista, dialogaba con nosotros.

'Sandino,' dijo una vez Carlos, 'es una especie de camino. Sería una ligereza reducirlo a la categoría de una efeméride más de disturbio anual. Creo que es importante estudiar su pensamiento.'

El leonés que vivió en México y que era algo así como delegado del Partido Socialista (del cual fue expulsado posteriormente) asustado replicó más o menos en los siguientes términos:

Carlos became an ant, a hammer, a typist and thence, everlasting. He spread subversive graffiti from wall to wall, and student and Party[3] newspapers from house to house. Almost immediately *El Universitario* was published, with fat headlines and in two colours, which gave statistical data without metaphors: 250,000 children of school age without schools or teachers (now there are 400,000); only 5% tax charged to mining companies on the gold they exported; these same companies exempt from taxes on agricultural and mining machinery, cars, electrical appliances etc. Figures: our country is paying foreigners to exploit our subsoil and take our gold. We are left with the coughing.

IV

At this time we were semi-recruited by the Socialist Party and Carlos led the first Marxist cell of Nicaraguan university students: Silvio Mayorga was one of the three militants. A man from León who lived in Mexico — we never knew whether he was a 'cowboy' or a Marxist militant — came to talk to us.

'Sandino,' Carlos said one day, 'is a sort of road. It would be trivial to reduce him to just another anniversary party. I think it is important to study his thought.'

The man from León who lived in Mexico and who was some sort of delegate of the Socialist Party (from which he was later expelled) was astonished and replied more or less as follows:

---

3.   The Nicaraguan Socialist Party (PSN), which Carlos joined in July 1955, but left when he no longer agreed that change could be brought about by reformist means.

'¿Un camino? ¡Eso es poesía! No olviden lo sospechoso de cierta exaltación que han hecho de ese guerrillero los ideólogos burgueses. Sandino luchó contra la ocupación extranjera, no contra el imperialismo. No llegó a ser Zapata, es decir: no planteó el problema de la tierra.'

Carlos expresó sus dudas ante esos argumentos. Se propuso investigar más a fondo el pensamiento de Sandino. Recuerdo la alegría y la severidad de sus violentos ademanes cuando llevó el libro *El Calvario de las Segovias*, en el que se pretende denigrar la figura del héroe inmortal. Este fue el primer elemento bibliográfico antes de conocer *Sandino: o la Tragedia de un Pueblo*, del honesto historiador Sofonías Salvatierra; el libro de un español de nombre largo e irrecordable; el escrito por Calderón Ramírez, y finalmente la obra de Selser. Con rigor y constancia, Carlos escribía notas, entresacaba frases de las variadas y ricas epístolas de Sandino. En esos apuntes se gestó *Ideario Sandinista*, cartilla de primeros conceptos que circula entre la militancia del FSLN.

V

Carlos viajó en 1957 a Moscú, como delegado del Partido Socialista a un Congreso Mundial de la Juventud. Desde una ciudad europea, Praga, escribía con lealtad conmovedora a su madre. Aprendí de memoria, pese a que la tengo renga, el contenido de uno de esos mensajes llenos de ternura:

> Estoy casi feliz, mamá, rodeado de muchachos alegres, de palabras nuevas; de ciudades bellas, inmensas, cordiales; nos llamamos unos a otros compañeros, aunque yo quisiera llamarlos hermanos. Casi feliz digo, porque usted

'A road? That's poetry! Don't forget the suspect way in which bourgeois ideologists have exalted that guerrilla. Sandino fought against foreign occupation, not imperialism. He did not become a Zapata, that is: he did not raise the land problem.'

Carlos expressed his doubts about these arguments. He decided to go more deeply into Sandino's thought. I remember the joy and severity of his violent reactions when he got the book *The Calvary of the Segovias*, which runs down our immortal hero. This was the first book we had before we discovered *Sandino or the Tragedy of a People,* by the honest historian Sofonías Salvatierra; a book by a Spaniard with a long name, difficult to remember; Calderón Ramírez' book, and finally Selser's work. Rigorously and persistently Carlos wrote notes, picked out phrases from Sandino's rich and varied letters. This work led to the birth of the *Ideario Sandinista*, a handbook which is circulated among FSLN militants.

V

In 1957 Carlos travelled to Moscow, as a Socialist Party delegate to a World Youth Congress. From a European city, Prague, he wrote feelingly to his mother. Although my memory is shaky, I learnt one of these loving messages by heart:

> I am almost happy, mama; surrounded by happy young people, new words; huge, beautiful, welcoming cities. We call each other comrades, even though I would prefer to call them brothers. I said almost happy, because you are not with me, so that I can give you a hug and share these

no está a mi lado para abrazarla y compartir estos momentos de claridad y asombro.

Cuando regresó a Nicaragua, escribió *Un Nicaragüense en Moscú*, en el que recoge sus experiencias, con la rectitud de siempre y lenguaje limpio, ameno, correcto.

En la Universidad es el delegado permanente de las subversiones elementales pre-Frente; dirigente de las asambleas estudiantiles, en los organismos universitarios, en las calles; organiza la primera huelga estudiantil a nivel nacional, que incluyó escuelas primarias, con paros prorrogables de 48 horas. 'Consignas de Moscú,' decía *Novedades*. La huelga era para rescatar de la cárcel a varios profesores y un estudiante injustamente condenados por un Consejo de Guerra.

En la Universidad agita; en los barrios de León organiza comités populares para demandas reivindicativas que, como suele ocurrir, se transforman en inquietudes políticas.

VI

En 1957, funda 'Nueva Nicaragua', movimiento que arranca torpe e inhibido. Es sin embargo, el primer paso de un grupo que intenta caminar hacia el sol, por los subterráneos de la clandestinidad.

El movimiento toma la iniciativa de una editorial, Nueva Nicaragua, que publica las obras de Selser y algunos escritos revolucionarios.

Este esfuerzo, tan difícil en aquel momento, revistió una excepcional importancia si se considera el aislamiento cultural e ideológico — muralla construida con paciencia patriarcal y oligarquía desde la independencia de la colonia española y que fue subrayada con palabras gruesas,

moments of clarity and astonishment.

When he returned to Nicaragua he wrote *A Nicaraguan in Moscow*, describing his experiences with his usual honesty in clear, graceful and apposite language.

In the University he became the permanent delegate of the pre-*Frente* groups; leader of student gatherings in university organisations and in the streets. He organised the first national student strike, which included primary schools, with class closures alternating in forty-eight hour shifts. 'Orders from Moscow,' said *Novedades*.[4] The strike was to liberate a number of teachers and a student unjustly sentenced by a military court.

In the University he agitated; in the *barrios* of León he organised people's committees to demand improvements, which as usual, soon became political demands.

VI

In 1957 he founded 'New Nicaragua' (MNN),[5] a movement whose beginnings were slow and halting. Nevertheless it was the first step of a group who intended to walk towards the sun, along clandestine paths.

The movement set up a publishing house called New Nicaragua, which published the works of Selser and some revolutionary writings.

This effort, which was so difficult at the time, was exceptionally important considering the cultural and ideological isolation which had been imposed on the Nicaraguan people. This was a wall built with patriarchal

---

4.   Newspaper controlled by Somoza.
5.   In fact the New Nicaragua Movement was not founded until 1961.

bayonetas y medidas legales por el fundador de la dinastía somocista — a que ha sido sometido el pueblo nicaragüense. El aislamiento fue tan cerrado y mezquino, que cuando el autor de estas líneas llegó a la Universidad y se juntó con un grupo de estudiantes — que después fueron rectores y banqueros — creyó, como los otros, que Haya de la Torre era revolucionario marxista y que en Nicaragua no existía un partido de la clase obrera. Claro está que nadie movió por esa época ni un miserable terrón de azúcar para atraerse a los estudiantes. Fue unos cuatro años más tarde que el Partido Socialista se percató de la existencia de los estudiantes, aproximadamente cuando Carlos llega a la Universidad. Carlos señalaba, posteriormente, con justa razón, que el proceso actual revolucionario en Nicaragua se inicia más por vergüenza que por conciencia.

La victoria de la lucha armada en Cuba, más que una alegría, es el descorrer de innumerables cortinas, fogonazo que alumbra más allá de los dogmas ingenuos y aburridos del momento. La revolución cubana fue, ciertamente, un escalofrío de terror para las clases dominantes de América Latina y un violento atropello a las de repente tristes reliquias con las que habíamos iniciado nuestros altares. Fidel fue para nosotros la resurrección de Sandino, la respuesta a nuestras reservas, la justificación de los sueños de las herejías de unas horas atrás.

VII

Salimos del país y se organiza en Costa Rica 'Juventud Revolucionaria Nicaragüense'. Carlos viaja de San José a la zona bananera costarricense — territorio norteamericano habitado por nicaragüenses y donde viven algunos ticos —

and oligarchic patience since the time of independence from Spain, reinforced by tough talk, bayonets and legal measures by the founder of the Somoza dynasty. This isolation was so complete and baleful that when the author of these lines arrived at the University and joined a group of students − who since then have become rectors and bankers − he believed, like the others, that Haya de la Torre[6] was a revolutionary Marxist and that no working class party existed in Nicaragua. At that time no one was prepared to offer even one stingy sugar cube to attract students. It was about four years later when the Socialist Party realised the existence of students, approximately when Carlos arrived at University. Later Carlos remarked rightly that the current revolutionary process in Nicaragua arose more out of shame than awareness.

The victory of the armed struggle in Cuba was more than a great joy. It was the drawing back of many curtains, a bonfire shining out beyond the simplistic well-worn dogmas of the moment. The Cuban Revolution certainly caused a shudder of terror throughout the Latin American ruling classes and a violent shake-up of the suddenly dismal relics with which we had set up our altars. For us Fidel was the resurrection of Sandino, the answer to our doubts, the justification for the dreams so recently dismissed as heresies.

VII

We left the country and the 'Nicaraguan Revolutionary Youth' (JRN) was set up in Costa Rica. Carlos travelled from San José to the Costa Rican banana zone − North

---

6.   Peruvian populist leader and social democrat.

de la casa donde estamos refugiados en San José, a los barrios donde nuestros compatriotas remiendan zapatos y nostalgias. Junto a él está, como antes y después, Silvio Mayorga, héroe y mártir de Pancasán.

Viaja a Guatemala y Venezuela; se introduce, por primera vez clandestino, a Nicaragua. Pretende, aún novato, contribuir desde la clandestinidad para darle un nuevo contenido a 'Juventud Patriótica', sobre cuya militancia tiene gran ascendiente. El Partido Socialista, por supuesto, se opone a semejante audacia y publica una nota social, en el semanario de siempre, en el que se anuncia la llegada al país 'del joven y valiente luchador estudiantil, Carlos Fonseca'. Inmediatamente se le captura y expulsa del territorio nacional, en avión expreso de la Fuerza Aérea, hacia Guatemala. De Guatemala se escabulle hasta México; en este país conoce al Profesor Edelberto Torres por el que siempre tuvo un particular afecto, el cual todos hemos compartido. El Profesor Torres escribe un libro sobre Darío — conocido y apreciado entre los intelectuales de habla hispana — y lo dedica a Carlos.

De México parte en 1959 hacia Honduras e ingresa en la columna que es masacrada a mansalva en El Chaparral, por fuerzas conjuntas de los ejércitos hondureños y nicaragüenses: por la CONDECA que aún no tenía siglas. La jefatura de la operación se ubica en la Embajada Norteamericana de Tegucigalpa. Una bala de carabina M-1 le atraviesa el pulmón. Como no se queja, los gorilas hondureños lo creen muerto. Casi lo entierran. Tampoco se queja en el doloroso trayecto hacia Tegucigalpa.

American territory, inhabited by Nicaraguans and a few Costa Ricans — from the house where we were staying in San José to the *barrios* where our compatriots were cobbling shoes and dreams. As in previous and subsequent journeys, his travelling companion was Silvio Mayorga, the hero and martyr of Pancasán.

Carlos travelled to Guatemala and Venezuela; for the first time he made a clandestine trip to Nicaragua. Even though he was a novice, he wanted to give some input to the 'Patriotic Youth' (JP), as he had a strong influence over their militants. Of course the Socialist Party opposed such audacity and published a social note in their weekly paper announcing the arrival in the country of 'the young and brave student campaigner Carlos Fonseca'. He was immediately captured and expelled from Nicaragua, on an Air Force plane to Guatemala. From Guatemala he managed to reach Mexico. Here he met Professor Edelberto Torres, for whom he always had a special affection, which we all shared. Professor Torres wrote a book on Darío, which became well known and respected by Spanish-speaking intellectuals, and dedicated it to Carlos.

Carlos left Mexico in 1959 for Honduras and joined the column which was savagely massacred in El Chapparal by the combined forces of the Honduran and Nicaraguan armies: the precursor of the future CONDECA.[7] The operation's headquarters were in the North American Embassy in Tegucigalpa. A bullet from an M-1 rifle pierced his lung. As he did not complain, the Honduran gorillas believed he was dead. They nearly buried him. Neither did he complain on the painful journey to Tegucigalpa.

---

7. Central American Defence Council, established by the US in 1964 to co-ordinate counter-insurgency activities in the region.

Silvio y yo estábamos en una cafetería en San José cuando el doctor Enrique Lacayo Farfán, un hombre honesto, nos llevó la noticia de su 'muerte'.

Me puse a llorar a moco tendido (ahora te lo puedo decir, Carlos), y un tico dijo: 'Miren a ese joven, está llorando como un güila.' Silvio que también lloraba, remachó: 'No seas pendejo.' Carlos sólo estaba herido, aunque de gravedad. Antes de los sucesos de El Chaparral había llamado por teléfono urgiéndonos a que nos presentáramos en Tegucigalpa.

'¿Pero cómo,' le dije, 'si no tenemos dinero?'

'Espero,' respondió, 'que tengan la suficiente imaginación para llegar aunque sea nadando.'

Algunos esfuerzos estábamos haciendo para marchar a Honduras, cuando se apareció un delegado de Somarriba, el Jefe de la Columna, que prometió integrarnos a la columna de refuerzo, lacrada, desde luego, de pretérito imperfecto.

VIII

Volvimos a encontrar a Carlos en Cuba. En La Habana se vinculó estrecha y fraternalmente con Tamara Bunke (Tania, muerta heroicamente en Bolivia); hizo amistad con el Comandante Guevara.

Silvio fue a Caracas y llevó a Cuba a un grupo de nicaragüenses; en las jubilosas calles de La Habana transitaba alegremente otro número de compatriotas. Ellos fueron los primeros guerrilleros sandinistas en las jornadas de Bocay y Río Coco.

Carlos marchó a Honduras a preparar condiciones favorables para nuestro regreso. En el mes de julio de 1961, en la ciudad de Tegucigalpa, con la presencia de

Silvio and I were in a cafe in San José when Doctor Enrique Lacayo Farfán, a decent man, brought us news of his 'death'.

I burst out crying and the tears poured down my cheeks (now I can tell you, Carlos) and a Costa Rican said: 'Look at that boy crying like a booby.' Silvio, who was crying too, retorted: 'Don't be daft.' Carlos was only wounded, but seriously. Before the events of El Chaparral he had telephoned us, urging us to present ourselves in Tegucigalpa.

'But how can we,' I asked him, 'if we have no money?'

'I hope,' he replied, 'you will have enough imagination to get there, even if you have to swim.'

We were trying to leave for Honduras, when a delegate of Somarriba appeared, the leader of the Column. He promised to put us into the reinforcement column, relegated by then, of course, to the past imperfect.

VIII

We met Carlos again in Cuba. In Havana he became close friends with Tamara Burke (Tania died heroically in Bolivia). He also became friends with Comandante Guevara.

Silvio went to Caracas and brought a group of Nicaraguans to Cuba. Other Nicaraguans were already celebrating in Havana's joyful streets. These were the first Sandinista guerrillas in the days of Bocay and Río Coco.

Carlos went off to Honduras to prepare favourable conditions for our return. In the month of July 1961, in the city of Tegucigalpa, in the presence of Carlos Fonseca,

Carlos Fonseca, Silvio Mayorga, y el suscrito, se funda el Frente Sandinista de Liberación Nacional.

Los primeros militantes del FSLN fueron Santos López, Jorge Navarro, Rigoberto Cruz, Francisco Buitrago, Faustino Ruiz, José Benito Escobar, Víctor Tirado y Germán Pomares.

El nombre de la organización lo sugiere, lo pelea y lo gana Carlos.

IX

En 1962, la naciente organización revolucionaria junta en las márgenes del Río Patuca, Honduras, 60 hombres que permanecen casi un año entrenándose en la selva, acosados de pájaros, venados, ríos caudalosos y garrapatas.

Los primeros en hacer incursiones al Río Patuca, donde se entrenó la columna guerrillera, fueron Carlos Fonseca y el Coronel Santos López.

Se juntan, de este modo, dos generaciones de nicaragüenses sellados por la presencia histórica del pensamiento sandinista. El Coronel Santos López fue integrante del 'Coro de Angeles', unidad de combate en la guerra de Sandino, especializada en adolescencia y en acciones comando; niños violentos y dulces, expertos en conquistar objetivos militares difíciles y sonrisas de muchachas, que llegaban a citas de confidencias conspirativas y amorosas a maquillarse con el agua de los riachuelos y a vigilar las marchas del enemigo.

La relación entre Carlos Fonseca y el Coronel Santos López no fue casual. Las viejas y nuevas generaciones sandinistas se buscaron en medio de las tinieblas hasta detectarse en el momento político y económico justo. Los viejos sandinistas nos transmitieron sus experiencias que

Silvio Mayorga and the present writer, the Sandinista National Liberation Front was founded.

The first FSLN militants were Santos López, Jorge Navarro, Rigoberto Cruz, Francisco Buitrago, Faustino Ruiz, José Benito Escobar, Víctor Tirado and Germán Pomares.

The organisation's name was suggested, fought for and won by Carlos.

IX

In 1962 the new-born revolutionary organisation gathered sixty men on the banks of the River Patuca, Honduras, who remained there for about a year training in the jungle, living with birds, deer, rushing rivers and plagued by ticks.

The first to explore the River Patuca, where the guerrilla column trained, were Carlos Fonseca and Colonel Santos López.

Thus two generations of Nicaraguans were linked together by the historical presence of Sandino's thought. Colonel Santos López was a member of the 'Choir of Angels' a combat unit in Sandino's war − adolescents specialising in commando attacks. They were sweet, violent boys, expert in attaining difficult military objectives and smiles from girls, who would turn up for conspiratorial or amorous rendezvous, with water from a stream as their only make-up and on the lookout for enemy movements.

The relationship between Carlos and Colonel Santos López was no coincidence. The old and new generations of Sandinistas sought each other out in the darkness until they found themselves at the right political and economic moment. The older Sandinistas passed on their experiences, which fell upon soil hungry for the seeds of new ideas. In

cayeron en un terreno hambriento de semillas y nuevas perspectivas. En verdad lo que ocurrió fue un desplazamiento del conocimiento escrito sobre la lucha de Sandino a la carne, los huesos y las palabras de los veteranos sobrevivientes.

Poco después llegan al Patuca los primeros militantes del FSLN: Víctor Tirado y Germán Pomares, entre los actuales sobrevivientes; Faustino Ruiz, Modesto Duarte, Francisco Buitrago, Rigoberto Cruz, Mauricio Córdoba y Silvio Mayorga, entre los caídos. Con el señor Guerrero tuvimos serias contradicciones que impidieron la participación de Fonseca en la columna guerrillera. Se vio obligado a internarse clandestinamente en Nicaragua.

Los guerrilleros del Patuca incursionan posteriormente en las márgenes de los ríos Coco y Bocay, y tienen algunos encuentros con la Guardia Nacional. Aquellos hombres semidesnudos y desnutridos, tienen un día hambre; al día siguiente fatiga y hambre; y unos días más tarde, leshmaniasis (lepra de montaña), fatiga y hambre. El mando se turna cada semana: hace falta la presencia de un dirigente como Carlos.

Los guerrilleros se repliegan difícilmente hacia Honduras: desnudos, desarmados, al borde de la inanición y, cosa curiosa, cuando al fin se ha consolidado como responsable uno de los combatientes.

Durante los encuentros con el enemigo caen compañeros que siguen siendo puntos de referencia, entre la militancia sandinista, de generosidad, de heroísmo, de alegría y de sacrificio. Cómo no recordar en estos breves apuntes a Jorge Navarro — el alegre, optimista y severo 'Navarrito' — que nos hacía cosquillas con sus anécdotas y sacaba el jugo a nuestras reservas de energía en las horas difíciles.

fact, what happened was the passing on of the knowledge of Sandino's struggle, not only in words but written in the flesh and bones of the veteran survivors.

Shortly afterwards the first FSLN veterans arrived at the Patuca: Victor Tirado and Germán Pomares,[8] among those still surviving; Faustino Ruiz, Modesto Duarte, Francisco Buitrago, Rigoberto Cruz, Mauricio Córdoba and Silvio Mayorga among the fallen. We had serious disagreements with Mr Guerrero, which meant that Fonseca could not take part in the guerrilla column, because he had to make a clandestine journey inside Nicaragua.

The Patuca guerrillas later invaded the banks of the Rivers Coco and Bocay, and had several encounters with the National Guard. Those half-naked, underfed men, went hungry one day; next day went hungry and suffered exhaustion; and a few days later they suffered leshmaniasis (mountain leprosy), exhaustion and hunger. The leadership was rotated weekly; we needed a leader like Carlos.

The guerrillas withdrew with difficulty towards Honduras: naked, unarmed, on the point of collapse, and curiously, when one of the combatants had finally established himself as the one in charge.

During encounters with the enemy, comrades fell who continue to be looked up to as examples by Sandinista militants, for their generosity, heroism, joy and sacrifice. In these brief lines how can we fail to remember Jorge Navarro — the jolly, optimistic and severe 'Navarrito' — who tickled us with his stories and could squeeze out our last drop of energy at the most difficult times.

---

8. Germán Pomares, known as 'El Danto' ('The Tapir') was killed leading the attack on Jinotega on May 24th 1979, during the FSLN Final Offensive.

Cómo no ver, aún entre las cuatro paredes de esta celda, los gestos y las palabras de Faustino Ruiz 'El Cuje', quien no extendía una mano sino para dar algo, o no decía una palabra que no fuera certera como una flecha para llegar al corazón.

Francisco Buitrago y Modesto Duarte tuvieron una reyerta porque Chico quería que Modesto Duarte fuera el Jefe de una de las escuadras, y Modesto quería que lo fuera Chico. El Coronel Santos López tuvo que tomar una decisión bajo el techo de las cejas fruncidas de Modesto y los ojos sonrientes de Francisco; por supuesto, el designado fue Modesto.

Conocemos el caso de un compañero — cuyo nombre lamentablemente no recordamos — que simulaba comer para dar secretamente parte de su ración a los más débiles. Sólo quien conoce el hambre de los guerrilleros sabe lo que esto significa.

X

En el interior del país, concretamente en Managua y Matagalpa, Carlos organizó con Jorge Navarro — el que caminaba a pie para no gastar en bus, con 33.000 pesos de la organización en la bolsa — las primeras células sandinistas y el primer grupo armado en las montañas de Matagalpa (que fue detectado en Carateras).

Jorge Navarro, bajo la dirección de Fonseca, planifica y ejecuta el primer acto de recuperación en una sucursal bancaria: 35.000 córdobas que son enviados íntegros a la montaña. Jorge lee un mensaje en Radio Mundial — ocupada con entusiasta e inexperta violencia — redactado por Carlos. Navarro posteriormente se incorpora al grupo guerrillero del Bocay.

How, even within the four walls of this cell, can I fail to recall the behaviour and language of Faustino Ruiz, *El Cuje*, who never stretched out his hand without giving something, and never said a word that was not an arrow straight to the heart.

Francisco Buitrago and Modesto Duarte had a dispute because Chico wanted Modesto Duarte to be a squadron leader and Modesto wanted it to be Chico. Colonel Santos López had to take a decision, faced with Modesto's heavy frown and Francisco's smiling eyes; he had nominated Modesto, of course.

We know of a comrade — whose name we unfortunately cannot remember — who pretended to eat in order to give his ration to the weaker comrades. Only someone who knows how hungry guerrillas are can understand what this means.

X

Within the country, that is, in Managua and Matagalpa, together with Jorge Navarro — who went on foot to save the bus fare even when he had 33,000 pesos belonging to the organisation in his pocket — Carlos organised the first Sandinista cells and the first armed group in the Matagalpa mountains (which was detected in Carateras).

Under Fonseca's leadership, Jorge Navarro planned and carried out the first act of recovery from a bank branch: 35,000 córdobas all sent to the mountain. Jorge read out a message composed by Carlos on *Radio Mundial* — occupied with enthusiastic and inexpert violence. Later Navarro joined the Bocay guerrilla group.

XI

Carlos sostiene, en sus escritos, que la experiencia guerrillera de Bocay y Río Coco no fue un foco guerrillero; que el FSLN nació con vocación de clases explotadas a las cuales se ligó desde la placenta. En efecto, el FSLN extendió el calor de sus primeras manos a las fábricas, a los barrios, a la universidad, a las comarcas de Matagalpa, Managua, Ocotal y Chinandega. Cuando llegamos a Nicaragua, en compañía de Víctor Tirado, después de la jornada del '63, había en Managua tres células proletarias y repetidos contactos con la periferia de la ciudad. Silvio había llegado, cuando estábamos en la Patuca, a Chinandega, gracias a cierto trabajo político realizado en la zona de El Viejo. El grupo armado de Matagalpa no fue hijo de la casualidad; y en Wiwilí varias familias quedaban esperando la llegada de la columna guerrillera. Es cierto que la columna se desplazó hacia una zona desconocida y habitada por una reducida población marginada y sin perspectivas políticas, pero ese fue un error complementario de la dirección guerrillera que no desnaturaliza las indicaciones y prácticas clasistas de la joven organización revolucionaria.

Esta tesis fue confirmada — sostenía Carlos — ya que el FSLN sobrevivió a los duros reveses del '63 y '67, a diferencia de otros esfuerzos guerrilleros en América Latina que desaparecieron dejando tan sólo el recuerdo de sus huellas heroicas, después de ser derrotadas militarmente. El FSLN, por el contrario, se ha fortalecido, en términos políticos, a raíz de cada derrota militar. Es imposible comprender la supervivencia y desarrollo de la organización sandinista sin tener en cuenta la obvia arquitectura de sus raíces en los sectores sociales agredidos y explotados de nuestro país.

XI

In his writings Carlos maintained that the guerrilla experience at Bocay and the River Coco was not a guerrilla *foco*; that the FSLN was born for the defence of the exploited classes, to whom it had an umbilical link. Indeed, from the first, the FSLN warmly stretched out its hands to factories, city districts, the university, and outlying areas round Matagalpa, Managua, Ocotal and Chinandega. When Víctor Tirado and I arrived in Nicaragua after the events of '63, there were three proletarian cells in Managua and multiple contacts on the outskirts of the city. When we were on the banks of the Patuca, Silvio made it to Chinandega, thanks to some political work done in the area of El Viejo. The armed group in Matagalpa was not an accident; and in Wiwilí several families were expecting the arrival of the guerrilla column. It is true that the column went off into an unknown region with a small, marginalised and unpoliticised population, but this was a mistake made by the guerrilla leadership, which did not change the class bias and practices of the young revolutionary organisation.

This thesis was confirmed — Carlos maintained — by the fact that the FSLN survived the severe setbacks of '63 and '67, unlike other guerrilla movements in Latin America, which disappeared leaving only the memory of their heroic deeds, after they had been militarily defeated. On the other hand, the FSLN became stronger, in political terms, after every military defeat. It is impossible to understand the survival and development of the Sandinista organisation without taking into account its obvious roots in the exploited and battered social sectors of our country.

XII

A partir del año '63 se consolida la autoridad de Carlos Fonseca como dirigente del FSLN. El proceso militar del Río Coco y Bocay impuso un repliegue que nos condujo a darle particular importancia al trabajo en los barrios laterales de Managua y otras ciudades. Este trabajo, como se sabe, se realizó conjuntamente con el Partido Socialista y el fenecido 'Movilización Republicana'. En este trabajo predominó el estilo reivindicativo y discursero. Por fortuna, el FSLN no abandonó las montañas ni las comarcas.

El primero de cada mes, Carlos se reunía con Rigoberto Cruz (Pablo Ubeda) y otros cuadros, que hicieron significativos esfuerzos organizando campesinos en el Bijao, La Tronca y Uluse, regiones montañosas del departamento de Matagalpa: organismos sindicales pero también políticos que forjaron las condiciones básicas del actual movimiento guerrillero.

Decía Carlos que el movimiento en el Río Coco y Bocay fue la primera acción preparada por un grupo homogéneo en términos políticos. Fue — agregaba — una especie de tanteo del sector revolucionario.

Carlos indicaba, en algunos de sus escritos, que la derrota del Río Coco empujó al FSLN hacia posiciones revestidas de reformismo.

No se renunció a la lucha armada — aclara en *La Hora Cero* — pero se interrumpió por algún tiempo el trabajo práctico para continuar la preparación. El factor — agregaba en las mismas reflexiones — que influyó en esta debilidad, fue que la derrota del '63 coincidió con un descenso en la lucha antisomocista.

La dirección del FSLN no logró comprender en aquel instante que este descenso era un fenómeno parcial, ya que

XII

From the year '63 onwards, Carlos Fonseca's authority as leader of the FSLN was confirmed. The military process of the River Coco and Bocay was a setback which forced us to pay particular attention to work in the outlying *barrios* of Managua and other cities. As is well known, this work was done jointly with the Socialist Party and the now defunct 'Republican Mobilisation' (MR). This work was carried out mainly through debate and discussion. Fortunately, the FSLN did not abandon the mountains or the country districts.

On the first of each month Carlos met Rigoberto Cruz (Pablo Ubeda) and other cadres, who were making significant efforts to organise the peasants in Bijao, La Tronca and Uluse, mountainous regions of the department of Matagalpa, into unions, which were also political organisations forging the basic conditions for the ongoing guerrilla struggle.

Carlos said that the movement in the River Coco and Bocay was the first action developed by a group that was homogenous in political terms. It was − he added − a sort of testing ground for the revolutionary sector.

Carlos suggested, in some of his writings, that the River Coco defeat pushed the FSLN towards reformist positions.

The armed struggle was not given up − he explains in *Zero Hour* − but practical work was broken off for a time in order to continue preparing. The factor − he continued in the same reflections − which influenced this weakness, was that the defeat of '63 coincided with a falling off of the struggle against Somoza.

The FSLN leadership did not understand at the time that this falling off was a partial phenomenon, because

en esencia el rumbo de la lucha revolucionaria era de progreso, de tránsito hacia la maduración. En 1964-65, el FSLN destinó en la ciudad la casi totalidad de sus energías al trabajo legal entre las masas, particularmente en los barrios periféricos de Managua y León.

Por el contrario, se realiza intenso trabajo político formando bases de apoyo clandestinos en las áreas rurales y montañosas.

Artífice de estos trabajos fue el compañero Rigoberto Cruz (Pablo Ubeda), quien siendo obrero disfrazado de curandero, llegó a ser campesino en el modo de hablar, de poner los pies en la difícil geografía de Matagalpa y hasta de tirar piedritas en esas tertulias cuando muchachos y muchachas campesinos salen a encender los hachones de la luna. Desde el punto de vista de su concepción ideológica y política, Pablo Ubeda siguió siendo un obrero.

XIII

En 1965 Carlos fue capturado en un barrio lateral de Managua, junto con Víctor Tirado López. Condenado por la 'Ley Quintana', estuvo seis meses en la cárcel donde llegó a visitarlo una muchacha espigada y dulce que después fue su esposa. En la cárcel escribió el valiente documento *Yo Acuso*. Al cumplir condena se le desterró — de nuevo en avión expreso — a Guatemala. Fue confinado en El Petén, donde conoció e hizo amistad con el teniente Luis Turcios Lima, futuro comandante de las Fuerzas Armadas Revolucionarias de Guatemala.

Turcios le obsequió varios libros de táctica militar. Carlos escapó a México, donde contrajo matrimonio con María Haydee Terán. Su esposa e hijos están bajo la

essentially the direction of the revolutionary struggle was forwards, on the way towards maturity. In 1964-5, the FSLN devoted nearly all its energies to legal work among the masses in the cities, particularly in the outlying *barrios* of Managua and León.

On the other hand, there was also intense political work being done to build up clandestine support bases in the rural and mountain areas.

The comrade chiefly responsible for this work was Rigoberto Cruz (Pablo Ubeda), a worker who disguised himself as a folk doctor, learned to talk like a peasant and know his way through the difficult geography of Matagalpa. He even took part in the pebble-throwing games at those young peasant men and women's moonlight parties. Pablo Ubeda's ideological and political ideas continued to be those of a worker.

XIII

In 1965 Carlos was captured in an outlying *barrio* of Managua, together with Víctor Tirado López. Condemned by the 'Quintana Law' he spent six months in prison, where he was visited by a tall, gentle girl who later became his wife. In prison he wrote the brave document *I Accuse*. At the end of his sentence he was expelled − by express plane again − to Guatemala. He was confined in El Petén, where he met and became friends with Lieutenant Luis Turcios Lima, the future leader of Guatemala's Revolutionary Armed Forces (FAR).

Turcios gave him several books on military tactics. Carlos escaped to Mexico, where he married María Haydee Terán. His wife and children are living under the friendly

fraterna protección del pueblo cubano. Regresó a Nicaragua en 1966.

XIV

El proceso electoral y su culminación sangrienta del 22 de enero de 1967 definieron las diferencias con las agrupaciones políticas aliadas. Mientras el Partido Socialista Nicaragüense (PSN) y Movilización Republicana (MR) participan en el proceso electoral con parlantes, firmas al pie y encendidas exigencias de unidad con la oposición burguesa — que desde luego no fueron escuchadas — el FSLN traslada sus principales cuadros a la montaña y a la cabeza de ellos, como indiscutible jefe político y militar, se coloca Carlos Fonseca.

La guerrilla de Pancasán y Fila Grande le ponen una marca definitiva a nuestro destino político. Sandino ya no es una efemérides, un disturbio anual, sino una especie de camino.

En el año 1966, se dan pasos prácticos — dice Carlos en *La Hora Cero* — para reanudar la acción armada. Ese año el Frente Sandinista adquiere conciencia de la desviación en que había incurrido a raíz de los golpes de 1963, y procede a la preparación de la base guerrillera de Pancasán. Aunque esta preparación constituyó un progreso en cuanto a labor organizativa en comparación con el movimiento armado del FSLN en 1963, respecto a táctica política y militar no representó un progreso serio. Fue un notable progreso de organización, porque no fue ya la habitual preparación del movimiento armado en un país vecino, con la circunstancia de la lejanía de la observación del enemigo principal, sino que fue la preparación de un movimiento armado en montañas situadas en el propio centro del país.

protection of the Cuban people. He returned to Nicaragua in 1966.

XIV

The electoral process and its bloody culmination of 22nd January 1967 made clear the FSLN's differences with its allied political groups. Whereas the Nicaraguan Socialist Party (PSN) and the Republican Mobilisation (MR) took part in the electoral process with loudspeakers, signatures and exhortations to unite with the bourgeois opposition – which of course were disregarded – the FSLN transferred its principal cadres to the mountains and at their head as undisputed political and military leader, stood Carlos Fonseca.

The guerrilla struggle of Pancasán and Fila Grande set the seal on our political destiny. Now Sandino was not a passing memory, an anniversary, but a kind of road.

In 1966 practical steps were taken – says Carlos in *Zero Hour* – to renew armed action. In that year the Sandinista Front became aware of the deviation it had fallen into because of the blows it had suffered in 1963. So it proceeded to prepare the guerrilla base of Pancasán. Although these preparations did display some organisational progress compared to the FSLN's armed movement of 1963, it was not very substantial progress in terms of political and military tactics. It represented a progress in organisation, because it no longer resorted to the usual course of preparing an armed movement in a neighbouring country, with the disadvantage of distance from the principal enemy. It was the preparation of an armed movement in mountains situated in the very heart of our own country.

XV

A las seis de la tarde recibimos la noticia. Carlos se había perdido después de un encuentro con un juez de mesta. El guía que lo acompañaba no logró encontrarlo en la obscuridad. El violento intercambio de disparos hacía suponer que Carlos estaba herido o muerto. Nadie podía saberlo porque era de los heridos que no se quejan. La sola posibilidad de su muerte nos aplastó, no podía ser, ese lujo no, al menos en ese momento, ni nunca, estábamos demasiado tiernos, además el amigo, el hermano, el jefe ejemplar.

En el encuentro salió muerto un caballo y herido el juez de mesta. Carlos logró llegar hasta la casa de un campesino colaborador. Quince días después se apareció en el campamento, barbudo, flaco, regañón.

XVI

La derrota militar de Pancasán, que naturalmente impuso un nuevo repliegue, demostró que el FSLN era una respuesta histórica, la síntesis necesaria a más de cien años de lucha popular. La autoridad política del FSLN adquiere más significado si se considera que, a raíz de Pancasán, se inicia el reflujo de la lucha armada en América Latina: apenas unos días después del combate de Pancasán muere heroicamente en Bolivia el comandante Ernesto Guevara. Javier Heraud, poeta adolescente que dejó huellas en la literatura de su país — otro Leonel Rugama — cae 'entre pájaros y árboles' cumpliendo la promesa de un hermoso poema, en las montañas del Perú. Hugo Blanco y Héctor

XV

At six in the afternoon we received the news. Carlos was lost after an encounter with a district 'justice'.[9] The guide who was with him could not find him in the dark. The violent exchange of shots led us to suppose that Carlos was wounded or dead. Nobody knew for certain, because he was the sort not to complain if he was wounded. Even the possibility of his death devastated us. It was just too much, it could not be, not at this time, not ever. We were too weak to lose our friend, our brother, our exemplary leader.

In the encounter a horse was killed and the 'justice' wounded. Carlos managed to reach the house of a peasant collaborator. A fortnight later he appeared in our camp, bearded, thin and very cross.

XVI

The military defeat of Pancasán, which naturally forced us to retreat again, demonstrated that the FSLN was a historical response, the necessary synthesis of more than a hundred years of popular struggle. The political authority of the FSLN acquires more significance if we consider that Pancasán constituted the ebb tide of armed struggle in Latin America: just a few days after the battle of Pancasán, Comandante Ernesto Guevara died heroically in Bolivia. Javier Heraud, an adolescent poet who left his mark on the literature of his country — another Leonel Rugama — fell 'among birds and trees', fulfilling the promise of a beautiful

---

9. A *juez de mesta* was a local rural boss, a 'justice' with law-enforcement powers, who acted as a henchman to the dictator.

Béjar, dirigentes guerrilleros peruanos, son capturados por el ejército de ese país, liquidando una tentativa armada aparentemente prometedora. Turcios Lima ha muerto en Guatemala.

Es el duro momento en que lo difícil es el pan nuestro de cada circunstancia. Los dogmáticos y los vacilantes descubren, una vez más, la sonrisa irónica que se les había extraviado años atrás. Carlos no pierde los estribos, no abandona su armoniosa terquedad histórica. Sigue trabajando con paciencia, juntando voluntades, enfrentándose al peligro y a las contradicciones domésticas; depura el sentido de la crítica.

Pancasán significó, por otra parte, el final de los remanentes foquistas. En la misma zona guerrillera se realiza un trabajo que considera la existencia de factores extra guerrilleros. Se continúa el trabajo político en las regiones periféricas de Managua y otras ciudades, se atiende la actividad estudiantil y sindical, se establecen vinculaciones con dirigentes de los partidos políticos tradicionales, intelectuales y sacerdotes.

Después de Pancasán se inicia la acumulación de fuerzas en silencio que lentamente dibuja en barrios y áreas rurales una creciente estructura orgánica.

XVII

Todas las casas se quemaron. Cayó presa Lesbia que conocía el último escondrijo. Salimos a buscar con Velia un sitio cualquiera donde meternos: encontramos una casa abandonada, las ratas parecían gatos y los agujeros, ventanas. Carlos estiró sus largas piernas en el suelo; la única colcha se la dimos a Velia. Una semana después, teníamos cinco casas de seguridad en el barrio.

poem of his, in the mountains of Peru. Hugo Blanco and Héctor Béjar, Peruvian guerrilla leaders, were captured by the army of that country, which thus wiped out an apparently promising armed uprising. Turcios Lima had died in Guatemala.

These were hard times in which difficulty was our daily bread. The dogmatists and waverers recovered, once more, their ironical smile, which had been wiped from their faces a few years back. Carlos did not lose his head, he clung to his serene historical stubbornness. He went on working patiently, co-ordinating our efforts, facing danger and internal disputes. He sharpened his critical sense.

Pancasán also meant the end to the last remnants of *foquismo*. Even in the guerrilla areas, work was done taking into consideration other factors beside the guerrilla struggle. Political work continued in the outlying districts of Managua and other cities. Attention was paid to the organising of trade unions, students, links were established with leaders of the traditional political parties, intellectuals and priests.

From Pancasán onwards began the period of silent accumulation of forces. Slowly in city districts and rural areas a growing organic structure was being built up.

XVII

All our houses were discovered. They captured Lesbia, who knew the last of the hiding places. We went out with Velia to look for somewhere to stay. We found an abandoned house, the rats were like cats and the holes like windows. Carlos stretched out his long legs on the floor. We gave the only bed-cover to Velia. A week later we had five safe houses in the *barrio*.

XVIII

En 1969 se reorganiza la dirección del FSLN. Carlos es nombrado Secretario General; se publican *El Programa y los Estatutos*; Carlos escribe *La Hora Cero*. Viaja de Nicaragua a Costa Rica, empeñado en impulsar un nuevo proyecto guerrillero que insurge en Bijao y Zinica, pero es sorpresivamente capturado por la policía tica. Se le rescata por la fuerza en el conocido asalto a la cárcel de Alajuela, pero es recapturado. Carlos Agüero dirige la acción que logra, al fin, su libertad, y parte para Cuba, donde permanece algunos años, sin desvincularse de Nicaragua y el FSLN.

En Cuba escribe *Viva Sandino*, libro que aún no ha circulado en Nicaragua, y que es, sin duda, un serio análisis de nuestra desconocida dimensión histórica. En escrito publicado en la revista *Tricontinental*, lanza la consigna de organizar a las masas en toda la plenitud geográfica del país.

Así fue: el FSLN se pone pantalones largos para visitar montañas, caseríos, comarcas, barrios laterales, fábricas, universidades, institutos. Crecemos, tal vez, demasiado aprisa.

XIX

Carlos nos decía, en algunas de esas pláticas donde consumíamos café, cigarrillos y madrugadas, refiriéndose al papel de la clase obrera y los campesinos y de la pequeña burguesía:

> Desde que el FSLN dejó de ser una sigla — y aun antes — hemos sostenido que la clase obrera está destinada por la

XVIII

In 1969 the FSLN leadership was reorganised. Carlos was named Secretary General; *The Programme and Statutes* were published. Carlos wrote *Zero Hour*. He travelled from Nicaragua to Costa Rica, on a mission to give encouragement to a new guerrilla project being set up in Bijao and Zinica. The Costa Rican police captured him by surprise. He was rescued by force in the well known assault on the Alajuela prison, but he was recaptured. It was Carlos Agüero who led the action which finally succeeded in freeing him. After that Carlos Fonseca went to Cuba, where he remained for a few years, keeping in touch with Nicaragua and the FSLN.

In Cuba he wrote *Viva Sandino*, a book which has not yet been circulated in Nicaragua, and which is a serious analysis of our little known historical dimension. In an essay published in the *Tricontinental* review, he gave the word to organise the masses throughout the country.

And so it happened: the FSLN put on long trousers to visit mountains, farms, country districts, outlying *barrios*, factories, universities, institutes. We grew, perhaps too quickly.

XIX

In one of those conversations during which we consumed coffee, cigarettes and the small hours, Carlos said to us, with reference to the role of the working class and peasants and the small bourgeoisie:

Ever since the FSLN ceased to be just a set of initials — and even before — we have maintained that the working

historia a encabezar la revolución victoriosa y, lo que es más importante, a pesar de las limitaciones impuestas por el desarrollo económico del país, nuestra organización buscó siempre, y localizó con frecuencia, las fábricas y otros centros de producción; subestimar el papel de los campesinos — en este país de campesinos ultrajados, hambrientos, desposeídos, con tradiciones armadas — sería, en la práctica, renunciar a la violencia revolucionaria, buscar el tránsito fácil a la legalidad, rendirse al enemigo, dormirse sobre la sangre de nuestros mártires.

La clase obrera, por supuesto, no es una metáfora; lejos está de ser una abstracción. Existe en una geografía tangible y hasta ella se puede llegar por las calles cargadas de reivindicaciones insatisfechas de los barrios laterales. La realidad exige que, muchas veces, la ruta del cuadro político hacia el centro de producción pase por una área rural. La Dirección Nacional del FSLN ha sido exigente con los cuadros intermedios para que se dé atención especial a las fábricas y a los obreros también fuera de la fábrica, en los barrios. En una ocasión que revisábamos el origen social de nuestra militancia en un regional, la casi totalidad eran trabajadores de algún centro de producción.

El destacamento armado de las montañas — punta de vanguardia y garantía del proceso — tiene en sus filas importante porcentaje de obreros, independientemente de que la montaña significa proletarización. A elementos obreros que se han distinguido por su firmeza y capacidad, se les ubica como dirigentes de masas, como jefes de columnas, como responsables de regional o de zona.

La clase obrera — sostenía con parecidas palabras Fonseca — no ocupa espontáneamente la posición de vanguardia. La mayor o menor agilidad para que la clase

class is destined by history to lead the victorious revolution, and this, more importantly, despite the limitations imposed by the country's economic development. Our organisation always sought out and frequently homed in on factories and other production centres. However, to underestimate the role of the peasants — in a country which has an over-exploited, hungry and dispossessed peasantry, with a tradition of arms — would mean in practice renouncing revolutionary violence, seeking an easy transition to legality, surrendering to the enemy and falling asleep upon the blood of our martyrs.

Of course the working class is not a metaphor. It is far from being an abstraction. It exists in a tangible geography and can be reached along streets daubed with the unsatisfied demands of the outlying *barrios*. The reality of the situation required that often the political cadre's route to the production centre passed through a rural area. The National Leadership of the FSLN insisted that the intermediate cadres pay special attention to factories and also to workers outside factories, in their *barrios*. On one occasion when we reviewed the social background of our militants at a regional meeting, nearly all of them were workers in some production centre.

The armed mountain detachment — the vanguard and guarantee of the process — contained in its ranks an important percentage of workers, apart from the fact that the mountain meant proletarianisation. Worker elements who had distinguished themselves through their firmness and ability, were appointed mass leaders, chiefs of columns, or officers for a region or zone.

The working class — Carlos Fonseca maintained in similar language — does not spontaneously occupy the

obrera reconozca su papel histórico, depende de distintos factores: el desarrollo industrial, el nivel político de las masas, la capacidad de los revolucionarios.

El movimiento revolucionario organizado es, en última instancia, la energía que desata la participación consciente de la clase obrera.

XX

La niña de 11 años se moría, inflamada, con los ojos grandes, maduros como de adulta, nos dijo que no quería morir, estaba desnutrida. Carlos la miraba con el ceño fruncido; yo la tomé en los brazos mientras mi hermano se paseaba desesperado. La niña se apagó como un candil con una gota de gas y yo no podía limpiarme los ojos porque tenía ocupado los brazos mientras la mecía. Carlos se metió en su hamaca y se puso a fumar.

XXI

'En Nicaragua, por desgracia,' decía Carlos refiriéndose a un viejo dolor de cabeza, 'la pequeña burguesía es reaccionaria, ignorante políticamente hablando y mal inclinada. Quienes tienen en este país formación pequeña burguesa, se rajan fácilmente ante el enemigo, no soportan el rigor de las campañas guerrilleras; son incapaces de mantenerse dignos y solidarios en las duras, aunque se hacen pipí de tanta euforia en las maduras.'

Así es. Después de la acción del 27 de Diciembre, eran los revolucionarios más entusiastas del mundo. Con los reveses de El Sauce y Ocotal, el ardor revolucionario se convirtió en objeción, miraditas temerosas hacia atrás y

vanguard position. The greater or lesser speed with which the working class recognises its historical role depends on various factors: industrial development, the political level of the masses, the skill of the revolutionaries.

Ultimately, the organised revolutionary movement is the energy which unleashes the conscious participation of the working class.

XX

The eleven year old girl was dying. She was burning hot and her huge eyes, with their adult knowledge, told us she did not want to die. She was undernourished. Carlos looked at her frowning. I took her in my arms while my friend paced up and down in despair. The little girl went out like an oil lamp down to its last drop. I could not wipe my eyes, because my arms were full as I was rocking her. Carlos flung himself into his hammock and began to smoke.

XXI

'Unfortunately in Nicaragua,' said Carlos referring to an old headache, 'the petit bourgeoisie is reactionary, politically ignorant and ill-disposed. Those in this country with a petit bourgeois background, easily give in to the enemy, cannot endure the rigour of guerrilla campaigns. They are incapable of maintaining their dignity and solidarity when times are hard, although they piss themselves with euphoria, when the fruits of these times grow ripe.'

That's how it is. After the action of 27th December, they were the most enthusiastic revolutionaries in the world. With the setbacks of El Sauce and Ocotal, their

finalmente, maratón.

XXII

Carlos nos ordenó que cambiáramos de campamento. Llegamos a la orilla de una quebrada y nos instalamos en una pequeña cresta geográfica. Por la noche Silvio, Carlos y el Chelito Moreno tenían fiebre, vómitos y diarrea. Por la mañana les dimos cloranfenicol, tres días después llegó Sócrates, el médico y dijo que la indicación era correcta: los compañeros tenían paratifoidea.

XXIII

'Implacables en el combate, generosos en la victoria,' se dijo en un documento público sandinista. Esta sentencia sintetiza toda una concepción relativa a las contradicciones con el enemigo. Tan antigua como el FSLN; tan exacta al modo de ser, a la ilimitada generosidad de Carlos Fonseca.

'La victoria tiene un precio elevado y triste. La alegría total, por eso mismo es patrimonio de las generaciones futuras; por ellas es que hacemos la guerra,' nos decía.

Debemos, no obstante, evitar los sacrificios innecesarios, ahorrar lágrimas y sangre. Los soldados de la Guardia Nacional son, como individuos, parte de nuestro pueblo. Ciegos instrumentos, por desgracia, de los desalmados oligarcas y sus amos extranjeros. Si un soldado de la Guardia Nacional cae prisionero en nuestras manos, no sólo deberán respetarse su vida y dignidad, sino que es preciso tratarlo como uno de nuestros propios hermanos. Preferible es pecar de generosos y no de rigurosamente justos. Lo importante − como dijo alguna vez Fidel − es eliminar el pecado, dejando a salvo al pecador.

revolutionary ardour changed to carping, timid backward glances, and finally, an all-out marathon.

XXII

Carlos ordered us to change camps. We arrived at the bank of a stream and set up on a little hillock. During the night Silvio, Carlos and Chelito Moreno were feverish, with vomiting and diarrhoea. In the morning we gave them chloramphenicol. Three days later Sócrates, the doctor, arrived, and told us that our diagnosis was correct: our comrades had paratyphoid.

XXIII

'Implacable in combat, generous in victory,' as was said in a public Sandinista document. This phrase sums up our whole idea regarding the contradictions with the enemy. Old as the FSLN, and faithfully reflecting Carlos Fonseca's own limitless generosity.

'Victory has a high and distressing price. Total joy, is therefore the patrimony of future generations. We are making war for them,' he told us.

Nevertheless we must avoid unnecessary sacrifices, spare tears and blood. The National Guard soldiers, as individuals, belong to our people. Unfortunately they are blind instruments of the heartless oligarchies and their foreign masters. If a National Guard soldier is taken prisoner by us, not only should we respect his life and dignity, but we should treat him as one of our brothers. It is better to sin by being over-generous rather than too rigorously just. The important thing – as Fidel once said – is to get rid of the sin and save the sinner.

Algunos de los que, sin duda, se alegraron con su muerte le deben la vida a nuestro dirigente, que siempre tuvo en sus labios palabras disuasivas para contener medidas radicales en el orden de los castigos, inspiradas en la indignación, de la repugnancia por los crímenes y abusos del enemigo.

'Si nosotros nos dejamos guiar por nuestros sentimientos personales,' decía, 'por la cólera, por el impulso explicable de cobrar con la misma moneda, caeríamos en los pecados contra los cuales estamos luchando. Si queremos construir una sociedad habitada por hombres nuevos, ¿no tenemos que comportarnos como hombres nuevos? Si matamos, si ultrajamos a un prisionero, ¿en qué nos diferenciaríamos de nuestros enemigos?'

XXIV

No quiso que lo fusiláramos. El joven campesino había desertado llevándose el revólver y 50 córdobas. Llegamos al rancho de sus padres. La mamá nos dijo, perdónenlo por favor, fue una locura. Carlos dijo, déjenlo ir. El joven campesino se incorporó a la guerrilla de Zinica.

XXV

En sus últimos pronunciamientos escritos en la montaña, hace un llamado a la renovación de nuestro método de trabajo:

Determinados contrastes ayudan a expresar mejor ciertas ideas. Por ejemplo, hay tareas en el medio campesino que es imposible que las atienda un estudiante, aparte de que

46

Some of those who no doubt rejoiced at his death, owe their lives to our leader, who always spoke up against radical measures in the way of punishments, demanded by some out of disgust at the enemy's crimes and abuses.

'If we let ourselves be guided by our personal feelings,' he said, 'by anger and the understandable wish to give as good as we get, we would fall into the sins against which we are fighting. If we want to build a society inhabited by new human beings, shouldn't we behave like new human beings? If we kill, if we abuse a prisoner, how are we different from our enemies?'

XXIV

He did not want us to shoot him. The young peasant had deserted, taking with him the revolver and fifty córdobas. We arrived at his parents' cottage. His mother begged us, please forgive him, it was an act of madness. Carlos said, let him go. The young peasant joined the guerrilla movement in Zinica.

XXV

In his final words written in the mountains, Carlos appeals to us to review our methods of working:

Particular contrasts help us to express certain ideas better. For example, there are tasks to be done in the country which are impossible for a student to do, although there are proletarised students who do indispensable work in this

hay estudiantes proletarizados que en ese medio deben cumplir tareas indispensables. A la vez que en el medio universitario hay tareas que no las puede cumplir el militante que ha tenido una experiencia exclusivamente campesina. Esto independientemente de la importancia de que el militante, en cualquier lugar que esté, deba estar relacionado en alguna medida con la vida del pueblo trabajador.

Carlos contribuyó notablemente en la formación del militante sandinista. Se predicó con el ejemplo y la palabra, la fraternidad, la disciplina, el placer del sacrificio, la inapetencia de los apetitos egoístas. Es asombroso y emocionante ver como los jóvenes extrovertidos de un país que exporta palabras hermosas y agudas, acosados por la corrupción y el egoísmo, pueden ser serios, respetuosos, discretos, modestos, impecables, cantan y ríen en la plenitud de la fatiga, se sonrojan con el reconocimiento y la admiración de todos los pueblos del mundo.

A lo largo de todo un proceso el FSLN aprendió a colocar en el lugar exacto a sus militantes.

Una forma correcta de dirección, señalaba Carlos, descubre la parte positiva y fructífera de cada miembro para canalizarla a favor de la vida de la organización, al mismo tiempo que también sabe descubrir la parte negativa de los miembros para limitar el efecto que pueda tener en la vida de la organización.

Al mismo tiempo enfatizaba: no debemos ocultar las debilidades de la organización, a la vez que debemos cerrar los oídos ante la reciente insolencia de quienes sólo quieren ver un resultado negativo en la balanza del camino recorrido.

area. On the other hand there are tasks to be done in the university environment which cannot be done by the militant who has had exclusively rural experience. At the same time, it is important that, wherever he may be, the militant must be connected in some way with the lives of working people.

Carlos made a notable contribution to the training of Sandinista militants. By word and example he preached fellowship, discipline, self-sacrifice, the unpleasantness of selfish appetites. It is surprising and moving to see how the extrovert young people of a country which exports sharp and beautiful words, young people constantly assaulted by corruption and egoism, can be serious, respectful, discreet, modest, impeccable, sing and laugh during times of exhaustion, and blush when they receive the praise and admiration of all the peoples of the world.

After a long process the FSLN learnt to place its militants appropriately.

A correct form of leadership, said Carlos, discovers the positive and fruitful side of every member and channels it to serve the life of the organisation. At the same time it discovers the negative side of members so as to limit the effect this might have in the organisation's life.

At the same time he emphasised: while we should not hide the organisation's weaknesses, we should also close our ears to the recent insolence of those who see only negative results in what we have achieved so far.

XXVI

Germán Pomares ('El Danto') y yo entrenamos a un grupo de campesinos, varios muchachos y una muchacha. Aprendieron a desmontar y montar el Garand, la carabina M-1, la subametralladora M-3 y la pistola .45. Carlos llegó y nos dijo: 'También enséñenles a leer.'

XXVII

Al hacer referencia a la unidad del movimiento revolucionario, Carlos señalaba:

Según lo enseñan grandes experiencias de otros pueblos, la unidad de un movimiento revolucionario tiene la fuente de su vida en la igualdad fundamental de intereses, que anima por dentro entre los millares y millares de trabajadores asalariados y desposeídos en una sociedad.

No es negativo, es más bien positivo que surja toda una variedad de opiniones respecto a la posible solución de los problemas. Esto no es nuevo y se ha dado en otras luchas revolucionarias victoriosas, como también en procesos históricos que datan de la antigüedad. Desde el mismo texto de la *Ilíada* se ven las discrepancias que surgen dentro de un mismo bando combatiente por cierto que en este relato que narra el papel que combatientes envejecidos pueden desempeñar a favor de la armonía en el seno del propio bando.

Un aspecto no debidamente conocido del proceso insurreccional cubano, es la discusión muy aguda que se dio nada menos que hasta julio de 1958, respecto al papel que debía desempeñar la acción armada en la montaña.

XXVI

Germán Pomares ('*El Danto*') and I were training a group of peasants, some young men and one young woman. They were learning to load and unload the Garand, the M-1 rifle, the M-3 sub-machine gun and the .45 pistol. Carlos arrived and said to us: 'Also teach them to read.'

XXVII

With reference to the revolutionary movement's unity, Carlos said:

> According to what we learn from the great experiences of other peoples, the unity of a revolutionary movement has its life-source in the fundamental equality of interests, which drives the thousands and thousands of waged and dispossessed workers in a society.
>
> It is not negative but very positive that a whole variety of opinions should arise about possible solutions to the problems. This is not new and has happened in other victorious revolutionary struggles, as well as in historical processes dating from antiquity. Even in the text of the *Iliad* we see the discrepancies arising within one group of fighters, although of course the story tells the part veteran combatants can play to bring about harmony within the group.
>
> One aspect not sufficiently well known about the insurrection process in Cuba is the very sharp discussion, which continued right up to July 1958, regarding the role of armed action in the mountain.

XXVIII

Sobre el lenguaje entre compañeros, recomienda:

Hacemos lo posible por emplear un lenguaje persuasivo y fraternal, teniendo el cuidado al mismo tiempo, de mantenernos fieles a la objetividad, renunciando al empleo de calificativos, ya que estos últimos muchas veces sólo contribuyen a agravar los problemas en lugar de ser formas para resolverlos.

Finalmente, asegura:

Pese a las debilidades y errores que arrastramos, tenemos que decir que el balance logrado en veinte años, desde que reanudamos la decisión de luchar con las armas, el 21 de septiembre de 1956, es positivo; que es positivo el balance de la labor que durante tantos años ha realizado el Frente Sandinista. Es imposible simplificar todo un proceso, pero en aras de la claridad y la brevedad, contestemos la siguiente pregunta: ¿Qué manifiesta mejor que nada el balance positivo alcanzado? Lo manifiesta el acero que tocamos en el militante clandestino urbano y en el militante de la guerrilla rural.

Los grandes revolucionarios han dicho que una revolución vale por su capacidad para difundirse. Y en Nicaragua, a partir del reclutamiento de la primera choza campesina y de la primera casa urbana de seguridad en 1961, ha sido posible levantar una columna de combatientes de acero, que son el pavor de los rufianes adueñados de Nicaragua, y la única esperanza de un pueblo sumido largamente en el dolor. Sin embargo, ¿es suficiente logro el acero militante combativo forjado? No. Debemos responder de manera más completa a la pregunta de lo que es posible y de los medios a utilizar, a

XXVIII

On the language to be used between comrades Carlos recommends:

> We should do all we can to use friendly and persuasive language, while at the same time taking care to remain faithful to objectivity. We should give up calling people names, as these often only aggravate problems instead of resolving them.

He concludes:

> In spite of the weaknesses and errors with which we are lumbered, we can say that the balance achieved over twenty years since we made the decision to take up arms, on 21st September 1956, is positive. The balance of the work done throughout all those years by the Sandinista Front is positive. It is impossible to simplify a whole process, but for the sake of clarity and brevity, we answer the following question: What shows better than anything the positive balance attained? The steel in the underground urban militant and the rural guerrilla militant.
>
> The great revolutionaries have said that a revolution can be judged by its power to spread. And in Nicaragua, since we recruited the first peasant hut and the first urban safe house in 1961, we have managed to raise a column of combatants made of steel, who inspire terror in the ruffians ruling Nicaragua, and are the only hope for a people who have suffered so long. Nevertheless, is it sufficient to have forged combatants of steel? No. We must respond more fully to the question of what is possible and the means to use, on the basis of the organisation we have already built. If we do not respond to this, we run the risk that the steel may rust.

partir de la organización ya forjada. Si no respondemos a esta pregunta, se corre el riesgo de que el acero se herrumbre.

XXIX

No podía caminar. Tenía llagas en los pies y las uñas del dedo gordo del pie derecho encarnadas. Llegamos al campamento y Rigoberto lo examinó. El dedo estaba infectado y no teníamos anestesia. Carlos se metió un pañuelo en la boca; inmovilizamos el pie y Rigoberto, con una navaja, le sacó pus, uñas, algunos quejidos. Carlos sudaba y nosotros también. Qué descanso. La marcha se inició a las 4 horas del día siguiente, a paso lento, de jefe rengo, imposible. El chinito me dijo con voz dulce: 'Qué bruto que es el Comandante.'

XXX

Imposible es, para nosotros, hacer referencias explícitas sobre el pensamiento de Carlos Fonseca; mucho menos señalar citas de sus escritos − en revistas, folletos y libros, donde constan los criterios políticos de nuestro Secretario General − que no están, por razones obvias, al alcance de nuestras manos. Aclaramos, por honestidad literaria, que las palabras atribuidas en este escrito al compañero Carlos no son, en la mayoría de los casos, citas textuales. En ellas tratamos de reflejar el contenido − y en lo posible la forma − de su pensamiento. Fonseca expresó esas y otras ideas en distintos momentos de su ejemplar existencia, más correcta y claramente que nosotros.

XXIX

He could not walk. He had sores on his feet and his right-foot big toenail was inflamed. We arrived at the camp and Rigoberto examined him. The toe was infected and we had no anaesthetic. Carlos put a handkerchief in his mouth. We immobilised the foot and Rigoberto took a knife and extracted pus, toenail and a few cries. Carlos was sweating and so were we. Some rest! The march began at four o'clock the following day, slowly, with our leader limping and impossible. The Chinaman murmured to me: 'The Comandante is in a foul temper.'

XXX

It is impossible for us to make explicit references to Carlos Fonseca's thought, let alone quote from his writings – in magazines, pamphlets and books, where our Secretary General's political views are stated – because, for obvious reasons, they are unavailable to us. We should explain, for the sake of literary honesty, that the words attributed in this account to comrade Carlos are mostly not literal quotations. We have tried to reflect the content – and as much as possible the form – of his thinking. Fonseca expressed these and other ideas at different moments in his heroic life, more correctly and clearly than we can.

XXXI

Con el ejemplo de nuestro jefe desaparecido, hoy la revolución sandinista marcha hacia el fondo de un vigoroso resurgimiento. Nuestros sueños están rigurosamente confrontados con las respuestas de la historia. El optimismo sandinista es objetivo, desnudo como un caballo fresco. La revolución que parió a Fonseca es una madre que lleva en su vientre nuevas y definitivas respuestas: la victoria Sandino, la victoria sangre de Carlos, la victoria siempre, héroes y mártires.

Tal como decíamos recientemente en nuestros alegatos en la Corte Militar que nos investiga:

Hoy, para nosotros y para nuestro pueblo, el amanecer ha dejado de ser una tentación. Mañana, algún día, pronto, brillará un sol desconocido para iluminar la tierra que nos prometieron nuestros héroes y mártires; tierra con caudalosos ríos de leche y miel donde florecerán todos los frutos, menos el fruto de la discordia, y donde el hombre será hermano del hombre, y en la que reinarán el amor, la generosidad y el heroísmo, y a cuyas puertas nuestro pueblo será un ángel guardián que con una espada de fuego impedirá el retorno del egoísmo, la prepotencia, la soberbia, la corrupción, la violencia y la explotación cruel y agresiva de unos hombres contra otros.

Por eso luchamos, por eso se ha derramado la sangre de Augusto César Sandino, de Carlos Fonseca y de centenares de patriotas y revolucionarios nicaragüenses.

XXXI

With the example of our vanished leader, today the Sandinista Revolution is marching towards a vigorous resurrection. Our dreams are rigorously confronted with history's replies. Sandinista optimism is objective, unbridled as a fresh young horse. The revolution that gave birth to Fonseca is a mother who carries new and final answers in her womb: victory for Sandino, victory for the blood of Carlos, victory always, for our heroes and martyrs.

As we said recently in our evidence given to the Military Court investigating us:

> Today for us and our people, now the dawn's no fond illusion. Tomorrow, some day, soon, an unknown sun will shine, shedding light on the land our heroes and martyrs promised us; a land with rushing rivers of milk and honey, in which all fruits will flourish, except the fruit of discord, a land where people will be brothers and sisters, in which love, generosity and heroism will reign. At its gates our people will set a guardian angel with a flaming sword to prevent the return of selfishness, domination, arrogance, corruption, violence and the cruel, aggressive exploitation of some by others.

This is what we are fighting for, for this Augusto César Sandino, Carlos Fonseca and hundreds of Nicaraguan patriots and revolutionaries shed their blood.

XXXII

Nuestro hermano cayó combatiendo en encuentro fortuito. Poco a poco ha llegado hasta nosotros información acerca de las circunstancias de su muerte: caminaba, hacia el campamento de Modesto, un grupo de compañeros. Un poco más allá del crepúsculo, bajo la lluvia y en uno de esos caminos donde la tranquilidad es siempre sospechosa, se escuchan tres disparos de revólver. El grupo se retira a la espesura. Claudia, la hermosa compañera de Carlos Agüero, logra observar en blanco y negro los pasos alegres de un campesino. Todos escuchan los gritos: un sujeto embriagado de cususa, bebida alcohólica e inevitable que fabrican los habitantes de las montañas, seguramente 'juez de mesta' es el autor de los disparos.

Carlos decidió esperar veinticuatro horas y en el crepúsculo siguiente reiniciaron el camino. A la cabeza del grupo marchaba el guía, detrás Carlos y a la retaguardia de siete hombres, Claudia. Sonó un primer disparo de Garand y hubo un inmediato alboroto de pájaros; unos segundos antes de que la obscuridad fuera interrumpida por el fuego de un fusil ametralladora Carlos se tiende y dispara con su carabina M-1, ordenando al resto de la escuadra la retirada. Los combatientes se retiran a rastras a corta distancia. El estallido de numerosas granadas y un súbito silencio traducen la difícil verdad: nuestro jefe y fundador ha muerto.

Los guerrilleros permanecieron observando desde la espesura. Por la mañana hay inusitado movimiento de helicópteros. Se oyen risas y gritos. Llegan oficiales de alta graduación. Le cortan la cabeza a Carlos y se la llevan al tirano quien no podía convencerse de que aquel hombre

XXXII

Our brother died fighting in a casual skirmish. Little by little information has reached us about the circumstances of his death. A group of comrades were making their way towards Modesto's camp. Just after twilight, in the rain, on one of those paths whose quietness is always suspicious, they heard three revolver shots. The group withdrew to the undergrowth. Claudia, the beautiful *compañera* of Carlos Agüero, managed to distinguish the merry footsteps of a peasant. Everyone heard the shouts: someone drunk on grog, the usual alcoholic drink distilled by the mountain people. Obviously a 'district justice' must have fired the shots.

Carlos decided to wait twenty-four hours and the following evening they set out again. At the head of the group marched the guide with Carlos behind him, then seven men, with Claudia as the rearguard. The first shot rang out from a Garand and there was an immediate flutter and squawking of birds. A few seconds before machine gunfire shattered the darkness, Carlos lay down and started shooting with his M-1 rifle, ordering the rest of the squad to withdraw. Reluctantly they retreated a short distance. An explosion of grenades followed by a sudden silence told us the difficult truth: our chief and founder was dead.

The guerrillas remained on watch from the undergrowth. In the morning there was an unusual flurry of helicopters. Laughter and shouts were heard. High ranking officers arrived. They cut off Carlos's head[10] and took it to the tyrant, who could not be convinced that this man pursued

---

10.   After the triumph of the Revolution, the body was dug up for ceremonial reburial in Managua. It was intact.

perseguido por la leyenda y por el odio hubiera muerto.

Carlos murió con el fusil en la mano, con el corazón desbordando de amor hacia los hombres, con los ojos azules apuntando hacia el futuro.

Cuando los representantes de este sistema egoísta y brutal sean tristes y casi olvidadas referencias históricas; cuando nadie recuerde a los charlatanes, a los desertores; cuando los afiches polvosos, pálidos e insepultos de hoy estén reducidos a cenizas, las generaciones libres, alegres, generosas de mañana, recordarán a Carlos Fonseca.

El comandante de la cárcel Tipitapa llega hasta nuestra pequeña celda jubiloso, con *Novedades* en la mano, a darnos la noticia: murió Carlos Fonseca, nos dice. Nosotros respondimos, después de callar unos segundos: 'Se equivoca, Coronel, Carlos Fonseca es de los muertos que nunca mueren.' El Coronel nos dice: 'Definitivamente ustedes son increíbles.'

by legend and hatred was dead.

Carlos died with his gun in his hand, his heart overflowing with love for humanity, his blue eyes pointing towards the future.

When the representatives of this selfish and brutal system have become sad, almost forgotten names in history books; when nobody remembers the charlatans, the deserters; when today's dusty, fading, tattered posters are reduced to ashes, the generous, happy, and free generations of tomorrow will remember Carlos Fonseca.

The governor of Tipitapa prison came gleefully to our small cell, with *Novedades* in his hand, to give us the news: Carlos Fonseca was dead. We were silent for a few moments and then replied: 'No, Colonel, you are mistaken. Carlos Fonseca is one of the dead who never die.' The Colonel said to us: 'Really, you people are incredible.'

1965. CARLOS FONSECA AND MARÍA HAYDEE TERÁN AT THEIR WEDDING.

TWO SONGS[11]

Carlos Mejía Godoy

COMANDANTE CARLOS FONSECA
SANDINISTA HYMN

---

11.   Both these songs can be heard on the cassette *Guitarra Armada*, available from the Nicaragua Solidarity Campaign, Red Rose Club, 129 Seven Sisters Road, London N7 7QG (0171 272 9619). Both songs quote from *Carlos, Now the Dawn's no Fond Illusion*. On the cassette the song *Comandante Carlos Fonseca* is introduced by Tomás Borge speaking his own words.

COMANDANTE CARLOS FONSECA

INTRODUCCIÓN – HABLA TOMÁS BORGE:
Cuando estábamos en la cárcel llegó un oficial de la Guardia Nacional lleno de alegría para decirnos que Carlos Fonseca había muerto. Nosotros le respondimos: 'Carlos Fonseca es de los muertos que nunca mueren.'

Poseídas por el dios de la furia
y el demonio de la ternura,
salen de la cárcel mis palabras
hacia la lluvia.
Y sediento de luz te nombro hermano
en mis horas de aislamiento.
Vienes derribando los muros de la noche,
nítido inmenso.

ESTRIBILLO:

Comandante Carlos, Carlos Fonseca,
Tayacán, vencedor de la muerte,
novio de la patria roja y negra,
Nicaragua entera te grita: ¡Presente!

Cuando apareciste llegaste a nosotros
con tus miopes ojos azules intensos,
fuiste entonces el hermano
terco indeclinable sempiterno.
Fuiste mecanógrafo, hormiga, martillo
y al día siguiente de nuestro encuentro
vimos tus letreros subversivos
en todos los muros de nuestro pueblo.

COMANDANTE CARLOS FONSECA

INTRODUCTION – SPOKEN BY TOMÁS BORGE:
When we were in prison an officer of the National Guard came to us full of glee to tell us Carlos Fonseca was dead. We answered him: 'Carlos Fonseca is one of the dead who never die.'

Possessed by the god of fury
and the demon of tenderness,
my words go out from this prison
into the rain.
Thirsting for light I summon
you brother, here in my loneliness.
You knock down the walls of the night
with your dazzling shine.

CHORUS:

Comandante Carlos, Carlos Fonseca,
Tayacán,[12] death did not conquer,
bridegroom of the black and red country,
all Nicaragua proclaims you: Presente![13]

When you appeared among us
with your short-sighted intense blue eyes,
from then on you were our brother,
stubbornly firm in your courage.
You were a typist, an ant and a hammer
and on the day after our meeting,
we saw your subversive graffiti
on all the walls of our village.

---

12.   *Tayacán* is an Indian word meaning leader.
13.   'Present!' When the Sandinistas call out the names of their dead heroes, they greet with them with the response: 'Present!', as in a roll call.

Una bala en la selva de Zinica
penetró en tu recio corazón de santo,
y estalló tu sangre en nuestras vidas
como una gigante bomba de contacto.
Desbordante de amor hacia los hombres,
trinitaria roja tu pecho desnudo,
tus ojos azules generosos
apuntando firmes hacia el futuro.

Cuando los afiches del tirano
sean insepultas huellas de la escoria,
cuando los traidores y cobardes
sean referencias de una vieja historia,
las generaciones venideras
de la Nicaragua libre y luminosa
van a recordarte eternamente
con tu carabina disparando auroras.

A bullet in Zinica forest
struck you in your great heart
and your blood burst over our lives
like a giant explosion of contact.
Overflowing with love for your fellows
on your bare breast heartsease flowered,
and your kind blue eyes were set
on the future, still looked forward.

When the tyrant's tattered posters
are peeling relics of scorn
and cowards and traitors are merely
names that are dead and gone,
all the coming generations
in Nicaragua now shining and free
will remember and never forget you
whose gunshots were crack of dawn.

HIMNO DE LA UNIDAD SANDINISTA

Adelante, marchemos compañeros,
avancemos a la Revolución.
Nuestro pueblo es el dueño de su historia,
arquitecto de su liberación.
Combatientes de Frente Sandinista,
adelante, que es nuestro el porvenir.
Rojinegra bandera nos cobija,
Patria Libre, vencer o morir.

Los hijos de Sandino
ni se venden, ni se rinden.
Luchamos contra el Yanqui
enemigo de la humanidad.

Hoy el amanecer dejó de ser una tentación.
Mañana algún día surgirá un nuevo sol
que habrá de iluminar toda la tierra
que nos legaron los mártires y héroes
con caudalosos ríos de leche y miel.

Adelante, marchemos compañeros,
avancemos a la Revolución.
Nuestro pueblo es dueño de su historia,
arquitecto de su liberación.
Combatientes de Frente Sandinista,
adelante, que es nuestro el porvenir.
Rojinegra bandera nos cobija,
Patria Libre, vencer o morir.

SANDINISTA HYMN

Forward, keep going *compañeros*,
onward to Revolution, on.
Our people are the masters of their history
and makers of the freedom they have won.
Fighters in the Sandinista *Frente*,
forward, for the future ours shall be.
Black and red the flag that flies above us,
our country must be free: so win or die.

Sons and daughters of Sandino
don't surrender, don't sell out.
We're fighting the Yankee
enemy of humanity.

Today dawn ceased to be a fond illusion.
Tomorrow soon a new sun will arise,
shedding its bright light on all the land
bequeathed us by our heroes and our martyrs,
land of milk and honey, rushing rivers.

Forward, keep going *compañeros*,
onward to Revolution, on.
Our people are the masters of their history
and makers of the freedom they have won.
Fighters in the Sandinista *Frente*,
forward, for the future ours shall be.
Black and red the flag that flies above us,
our country must be free: so win or die.

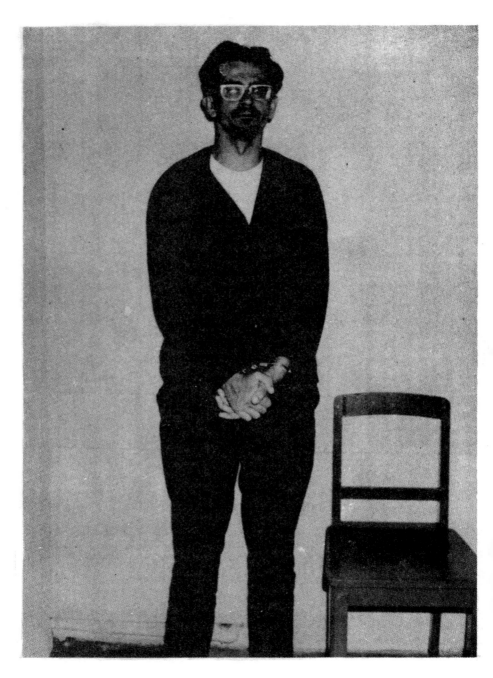

1969. CARLOS FONSECA HANDCUFFED IN PRISON IN COSTA RICA.

CHRONOLOGICAL NOTES BY TOMÁS BORGE

Tomás Borge reminds readers that these notes were written in prison and the dates recalled from memory.

1934

On 21st February 1934, with the murder of our national hero Augusto César Sandino and hundreds of patriots, North American imperialism and the liberal-conservative oligarchy brutally attack the popular and patriotic movement in our country. Since then our people have not found any other means of fighting back. In the country there is no leadership, no organisation, no revolutionary consciousness. The traditional parties dominate political activity in Nicaragua.

1944

The first left groups are formed in Nicaragua, following the line of the Secretary General of the US Communist Party, Earl Browder.

1956

On September 21st the national hero Rigoberto López Pérez executes the tyrant Anastasio Somoza García, 'so that Nicaragua might be again (or rather, become for the first time) a free country, without shame or blemish...'

1958

The veteran Sandinista Ramón Raudales resumes guerrilla action and dies fighting the National Guard.

1959

The victory of armed struggle in Cuba awakens the enthusiasm of the Nicaraguan people and stirs up the struggle against tyranny.

Air landing at Olama y Mollejones. Several dozen heavily armed cadres are captured by the National Guard. The former army captains, Victor Manuel Rivas and Napoleón Ubilla, take part in the expedition and are killed.

In the month of June the Rigoberto López Pérez

guerrilla column, which has benefited from the solidarity of Ernesto Che Guevara in its training, is brutally attacked in El Chaparral, a frontier point between Nicaragua and Honduras, by the armies of both countries. A number of Nicaraguans and Cubans die, and Carlos Fonseca is seriously wounded.

In protest against this massacre the students take to the streets of León on July 23rd. They are machine-gunned by the National Guard, four students are killed and more than a hundred wounded.

1960

Guerrilla movement in the mountains of Nicaragua. Those who fall in combat are: Chale Haslam, farmer; Manuel Díaz Sotelo, journalist; Julio Alonso, ex-soldier of the National Guard; Heriberto Reyes, veteran Sandinista.

Juventud Patriótica Nicaragüense (Nicaraguan Patriotic Youth) is organised inside the country and *Juventud Revolucionaria Nicaragüense* (Nicaraguan Revolutionary Youth) abroad.

1961

The Sandinista National Liberation Front is founded. On the shores of the River Patuca in Honduras, combatants join under the leadership of Colonel Santos López, the veteran Sandinista.

Guerrilla squads are organised in the urban areas, under the leadership of Carlos Fonseca and Jorge Navarro. The first worker and student cells are formed in Managua and León and the first peasant groups organised in Chinandega, Matagalpa, Estelí, Somoto and Ocotal.

1963

In March a guerrilla squad led by Jorge Navarro takes over *Radio Mundial* and broadcasts an FSLN proclamation, which denounces the meeting taking place in San José de Costa Rica between John Kennedy and the Central American presidents. The recently imposed puppet president René Schick and the dynasty's clan

member Luis Somoza attend from Nicaragua.

In May we bring off another action of economic recovery, when a Sandinista squad occupies the Bank of America in Managua.

On June 23rd the village of Raití is occupied by an FSLN guerrilla unit; the commissariats are expropriated and food and clothing are distributed to the population of the area. The village of Gualaquistán is taken. There is fighting in Sang Sang, where Silvio Mayorga is wounded, a National Guard officer and several soldiers are killed. Those who fall in these actions are: Jorge Navarro, Francisco Buitrago, Iván Sánchez, Boanerges Santamaría, Modesto Duarte and Faustino Ruiz. Pablo Ubeda, manages, with the help of local people, to reach Las Bayas in the department of Matagalpa, where he begins intensive and far-reaching work among the peasants.

1964

Work in the mountains is extended under the leadership of Rigoberto Cruz − the legendary Pablo Ubeda − with the support of Carlos Reyna, Fausto García and Carlos Tinoco. This work spreads to the departments of Matagalpa, Jinotega and Zelaya. Trade unions and Sandinista cells are set up in Uluse, El Bijao, La Tronca, Agua María, Cerro Colorado, Cuskaguas, Yaosca, El Carmen, Cubalí, Guaslala, El Garrobo, El Kun, El Naranjo, El Ocote, Fila Grande, Pancasán and El Tuma. Literacy schools are organised in the mountains and peasants are sent to Managua to be given revolutionary training.

1966

Armed actions are resumed. The Liberal Nationalist Party's Convention − at which Anastasio Somoza Debayle's candidacy for the presidency is announced − is sabotaged. Economic recoveries are carried out in many banks throughout the country. A group of Sandinistas led by Oscar Turcios take part, as a form of military training, in the Guatemalan guerrilla movement

headed by Luis Turcios Lima.

1967

The FSLN works to set up a guerrilla base in the Darío Mountains. The economic recoveries continue and the Sandinista Front publishes a communiqué denouncing the electoral farce.

On January 22nd an anti-Somoza demonstration is machine-gunned. More than four hundred people are killed.

In September the National Guard breaks through to the Darío Mountains. The peasant population is repressed. They torture and kill the peasant leaders Eufresinio Dávila, Eucadio Picado, Moisés Picado, Felipe Gaitán, Fermín Díaz and his five children. Armando Flores, a young Sandinista combatant, is flayed alive with a razor blade, sprinkled with salt and dies in agony.

After prolonged resistance, those who fall in combat are: Silvio Mayorga, Rigoberto Cruz, Francisco Moreno, Otto Casco, Fausto García, the guerrilla doctor Danilo Rosales, and Nicolas Sánchez (the 'Tiger of the Cerro Colorado').

In September the most infamous torturer of the age, Gonzalo Lacayo, is executed in Managua. The Sandinista Luciano Vílchez, known as the 'Lion of El Dorado', is murdered in prison. On November 4th Casimiro Sotelo, the important student leader and member of the FSLN Directorate, is captured in broad daylight, together with Edmundo Pérez, Hugo Medina and Roberto Amaya. When their bodies are handed over they show signs of torture.

1968

In April, David and René Tejada, former National Guard officers who had become FSLN militants, are captured. They are flogged by Somoza's personal aide, Major Oscar Morales. David dies as a result of the blows and his corpse is thrown into the smoking crater of the Santiago volcano, provoking world-wide protest.

1969

Political work is stepped up in the Matagalpa mountains and the cities of Managua, León and Estelí. Many intensive political and military training courses are set up.

In the Northern mountains, particularly in Yaosca, National Guard patrols, led by Corporal Miguel Tinoco, repress the peasant population. Murder, rape, torture, house-burning all increase. In Costa Rica, through the joint operations of the Costa Rican and Nicaraguan Security Forces, several Sandinista leaders are captured, including Carlos Fonseca, Oscar Turcios, Humberto Ortega, Henry Ruiz and Tomás Borge.

On July 15th the house of the national FSLN leader, Julio Buitrago, is detected and attacked by more than four hundred National Guardsmen, with artillery and air support. Julio Buitrago resists to the death, for more than three hours. It was the battle of one man against an army. As a result of this action, people said there might be men as heroic but none more heroic than Julio Buitrago. On the same day, in a similar operation Marco Antonio Rivera, Aníbal Castrillo and Alesio Blandón also fall in combat. These events arouse admiration and profound respect for the FSLN. Many young people ask to be admitted to the Sandinista ranks.

On December 23rd, two Sandinista squads attack the Alajuela barracks in Costa Rica, and manage to free Carlos Fonseca, but various armed confrontations with the repressive forces foil the action's success.

1970

A considerable number of Sandinistas, mostly peasants, gather in the mountainous region of El Bijao, in the department of Matagalpa.

On January 2nd a Sandinista squad, led by the poet Leonel Rugama, together with combatants Róger Nuñez and Mauricio Hernández, carry out an economic recovery raid on the bank branch of El Arbolito in Managua.

On January 15th they discover the safe house of Leonel Rugama — the best poet of his generation —, Roger Nuñez and Mauricio Hernández. More than three hundred National Guardsmen, helicopters and tanks appear. The three Sandinistas fight heroically with their primitive weapons. The rattle of machine gunfire and the tanks' booming cannon do not drown their war songs and combat shouts, until they die riddled with bullets among the smoking ruins. Thousands of people support the guerrillas by shouting: 'A free country or death!'

In the month of February on the anniversary of the murder of the national hero Augusto César Sandino, Sandinista squads place explosives in the houses of Somocista military and politicians. On the February 21st a guerrilla squad broadcasts an FSLN communiqué on *Radio Mundial.*

That same month the Pablo Ubeda column, camped near the River Waslala, is detected. Two hundred National Guardsmen reach the mountains and three patrols set out from different points for the guerrilla camp. On February 11th a patrol comprising forty National Guardsmen, approaching from Las Vallas, are held off by the Sandinista reserve, positioned at a short distance from the department. One of the enemy is wounded.

The camp is abandoned by the guerrillas and the women and children accompanying them. Most of the guerrillas regroup on El Bijao mountain, where they are joined by Oscar Turcios as leader.

The enemy sets up a vigilant watch and represses the peasant population. Local agents murder the Sandinista combatants Luis Cabo Hernández and Jesús Méndez, both peasants.

A National Guard patrol murder nineteen members of a family by the name of Moncada in Wamblán. In Kilambé they murder Alfonso Tórrez and two workers. They rape

two peasant girls, both called Martínez. Denounced by the landholder, Marcelino Castro, a number of young peasants are captured by a National Guard patrol and tortured to death at La Gloria near the El Carmen estate. They are all members of the Ramos family and their names are: Julio aged thirty-four; Toribio aged twenty-five; Doroteo aged eighteen; Julián aged fourteen and Daniel aged nine. In El Cuá they capture Juan Saturnino González and Juan Hernández López and take them up in a military plane. In Las Valles Juan Hernández Sánchez and Gabino Hernández Sánchez are murdered.

In El Cuá several old women are captured and tortured, including Venancia Hernández aged ninety-eight. They capture two peasant girls named Cándida Donaire Romero and Angela García and rape them. The leader of the repressive operations is the National Guard Captain Manuel Sandino, with Lieutenant Juan Lee Wong as his second in command.

In the city of León on April 3rd various Sandinista combatants are discovered by the National Guard chief of investigations. The guerrillas execute him. The enemy unleashes a repressive operation in the city. They discover the Sandinistas Luisa Amando Espinosa and Enrique Lorente, who fight to the death against enemy patrols supported by helicopters.

In the month of May the Sandinista combatant Igor Ubeda dies after wounding a National Guard mercenary guarding a bank which the guerrillas plan to attack.

In July in the city of Jinotega, the young peasant Sandinista Efrén Ortega is murdered while carrying out messenger duties.

In August, Sandinistas Edwin Meléndez, Orlando Castrillo and Noel Argüello are machine-gunned while on their way to make contact with the mountain.

In the city of Estelí various agents of repression are executed. Mainly in the mountains of the departments of

Matagalpa and Jinotega, district 'justices' are executed for denouncing peasant trade unionists.

On September 5th in an FSLN act of solidarity with the just cause of the Arab peoples, Sandinista combatant Patricio Argüello is mortally wounded when he tries, together with Palestinian guerrillas, to hijack a Zionist plane in French skies. A subsequent hijacking, also over Europe, in which Juan José Quezada takes part, succeeds in retrieving Argüello's body and freeing a Palestinian guerrillera.

1971

On October 21st, a commando hijacks a plane in Costa Rica, in which four Yankee businessmen of the United Fruit Company are travelling, and succeeds in freeing Sandinista leader Carlos Fonseca Amador and comrades Humberto Ortega, Plutarco Hernández and Rufo Marín. The Sandinista Fabián Rodríguez is murdered near the city of Matagalpa.

1974

The Juan José Quezada commando occupies the house of Doctor José María Castillo, a functionary of the Somoza regime. A party in honour the Yankee ambassador is being held in Castillo's house.

High government officials and members of the diplomatic corps are taken hostage. The commando, led by Eduardo Contreras, demands the liberation of Sandinista prisoners, five million US dollars, an increase in the minimum pay of National Guard soldiers and the publication in the press and on radio of two FSLN communiqués.

The regime agrees in essentials to these demands.

The action has worldwide repercussions and initiates a new stage of the struggle.

Guerrilla warfare in the mountains is stepped up under the leadership of Henry Ruiz and Carlos Agüero.

The repression becomes more widespread and intense.

Martial law is established and a permanent military court is set up.

1965. FROM LEFT TO RIGHT: CARLOS FONSECA, PROFESSOR EDELBERTO TORRES AND VÍCTOR TIRADO LÓPEZ.

CARLOS FONSECA 1936-1976
CHRONOLOGY[14]

1936-53

Carlos Fonseca is born on June 23rd 1936 in Matagalpa. He grows up with his mother, Justina Fonseca, a poor domestic servant. His father Fausto Amador is an accountant. From the age of nine Carlos does a variety of jobs to help his mother. He meets Tomás Borge as a child in Matagalpa, where they go to school. In 1953, he, Tomás and others begin studying literary and socialist classics, which they discover in a local bookshop. His political concerns draw him towards UNAP (Unión Nacional de Acción Popular: National Union for Popular Action), but he becomes disillusioned with them.

1954

He becomes a leading student activist in the Matagalpa Instituto Nacional del Norte, together with Francisco Buitrago.[15] In August they set up the magazine *Segovia* together.

1955

He receives a gold medal for being the Institute's best student. His thesis is entitled *El Capital y el Trabajo (Capital and Labour)*. In May he leaves for Managua, where he works as a librarian in the Institute Ramírez Goyena. In September he takes part in the patriotic march, organised by the Ramírez Goyena students, to San Jacinto, where the Nicaraguans defeated the self-proclaimed president of Nicaragua, 'filibuster' William Walker on September 14th 1856.

1956

He enrols as a law student at the University of León, and works with Tomás Borge as a correspondent for *La Prensa*. In

---

14. The principal source of this outline chronology of Carlos Fonseca's life is *Carlos: El Eslabón Vital — Cronología Básica de Carlos Fonseca, Jefe de la Revolución, 1936-1976* (Instituto de Estudio del Sandinismo: Managua 1985).

15. Francisco Buitrago was a co-founder of the New Nicaragua Movement (MNN), which developed into the FSLN. He fell in combat during the Raití Bocay guerrilla action in 1963.

July, Tomás, Silvio Mayorga[16] and Carlos set up the first Marxist cell of university students. On September 27th, following the execution of the dictator Somoza García by the poet Rigoberto López Pérez, Carlos and Tomás Borge are imprisoned by the National Guard, severely beaten and kept in solitary confinement. Carlos is released in Managua on November 14th.

1957

In the National Association of Students (ANE) Carlos speaks in support of the striking Corinto port-workers and trade union freedom. In July he travels to Costa Rica, where he meets his friend the poet Manolo Cuadra. On July 24th he travels to Moscow, where he takes part as a Nicaraguan Youth delegate in the Sixth World Youth Festival. In August he attends the Fourth World Youth Congress in Kiev, and in October, the Fourth World Trade Union Congress in Leipzig. On November 7th he attends the fortieth anniversary celebrations of the October Revolution in Red Square, Moscow. On December 16th on his return from the USSR, he is detained by the Security Forces (OSN) at Managua airport and interrogated in the Presidential Palace.

1958

In January he writes the pamphlet *Un Nicaragüense en Moscú (A Nicaraguan in Moscow)*, published in May. In July he organises student protests against the visit of Milton Eisenhower to Nicaragua. These protests manage to prevent Eisenhower receiving an honorary doctorate from the University. In October he is a member of a student delegation to Luis Somoza to demand the release of prisoners detained since the execution of Somoza García, who include Tomás Borge. In November he organises student demonstrations for the prisoners' release. On November 29th he is detained in the National Stadium with other students.

1959

The Cuban Revolution takes place in January. In March, together with Silvio Mayorga, Carlos organises the Nicaraguan

---

16.   Silvio Mayorga was a co-founder of the FSLN and a member of its National Directorate. He was killed at Pancasán on 27th August 1967.

Democratic Youth (JDN) to protest against the dictatorship. On April 8th he is expelled to Guatemala on a military aircraft. In May he leaves for Honduras to join the 'Rigoberto López Pérez' column, which is preparing to enter Nicaragua in a guerrilla action against the dictatorship. On June 24th the guerrilla column is attacked by Honduran and Nicaraguan military at El Chaparral and Carlos receives a serious lung injury. He is imprisoned but released by popular pressure from the Honduran people. His mother visits him in hospital in Tegucigalpa.

On July 23rd, following reports of his death, there is a large student demonstration in León, at which the National Guard opens fire on the demonstrators, killing four and wounding hundreds.

In September Carlos moves to Cuba to recover in the Calixto García Hospital. In November he goes to Costa Rica, joins the Nicaraguan Revolutionary Youth (JRN) and together with Silvio Mayorga and Tomás Borge, establishes contacts with Nicaraguan workers – including Adolfo García Barberena[17] – in the US banana plantations in Costa Rica.

1960

From February 20-22nd he and Silvio Mayorga are student representatives at the Nicaraguan Democratic Emigrants' conference in Venezuela, campaigning against the dictatorship. On March 4th he and Mayorga speak in the Central University of Venezuela and present their *Breve Análisis de la Lucha Popular contra la Dictadura de Somoza (Short Analysis of the Popular Struggle against the Somoza Dictatorship)*.

In June Carlos returns secretly to Nicaragua and establishes contacts with the Nicaraguan Patriotic Youth (JPN). On July 18th he is arrested by the Security Forces (OSN) in Managua and again expelled from the country, to be imprisoned in Poptún, in the El Petén region of Guatemala. There he meets Luis Augusto Turcios Lima, who later becomes leader of the Guatemalan guerrilla movement, Rebel Armed Forces (FAR).

---

17.   Adolfo García Barberena was killed in Nueva Guinea on May 17th 1979.

1961

Together with Tomás Borge, Silvio Mayorga and others, he founds the New Nicaragua Movement (MNN), the predecessor to the FSLN. In July he meets Tomás Borge, Silvio Mayorga and Noel Guerrero (who subsequently leaves the FSLN) in Tegucigalpa, Honduras, and proposes the name Sandinista National Liberation Front (FSLN) for the new revolutionary organisation. This is regarded as the official foundation of the FSLN.

1962

On his return from Cuba in June, Carlos does reconnaissance work to explore the Rivers Huayata and Patuca on the Nicaraguan border with Honduras, in preparation for the guerrilla activities in the Raití-Bocay region in 1963. In September a communiqué denouncing imperialist aggression against Cuba is signed by the Sandinista National Liberation Front, using this name. In December he leaves the border region and secretly enters Nicaragua to build up urban bases.

1963

He directs FSLN operations inside Nicaragua and promotes the publication of the FSLN paper *Trinchera*. During the year he makes several trips abroad on FSLN business.

In March an FSLN squad takes over *Radio Mundial* in Managua and broadcasts a denunciation of President Kennedy's meeting with the Central American presidents. On May 31st the FSLN conducts an 'economic recovery' raid on the Bank of America in Managua.

From July to October the FSLN mount their first guerrilla actions inside Nicaragua in the Raití Bocay region near the northern border.

1964

On June 29th Carlos and Victor Tirado López are captured by the Security Forces (OSN) in the San Luis *barrio* of Managua. In La Aviación prison he writes the manifesto *Desde la Cárcel Yo Acuso a la Dictadura (From Prison I Accuse the Dictatorship)*. On September 21st from cell number 13 of La Aviación prison, he issues the proclamation *Esta es la Verdad (This is the Truth)*.

1965

On January 6th Carlos is expelled for the third time to Guatemala. He escapes to Mexico and denounces the inhuman treatment he has suffered in a letter to the director of Managua *Radio Informaciones.*

In Mexico on April 1st he marries María Haydee Terán, followed by a religious ceremony on April 3rd.

In August he travels secretly to Costa Rica, doing organisational work for the FSLN and scholarly work on the Nicaraguan national poet Rubén Darío, in collaboration with Professor Edelberto Torres.

1966

In March he enters Nicaragua secretly to direct preparations for the new stage of armed struggle.

He works closely with Silvio Mayorga, Oscar Turcios,[18] Rigoberto Cruz ('Pablo Ubeda'),[19] Carlos Reyna,[20] José Benito Escobar,[21] Enrique Lorente,[22] Francisco Moreno,[23] Roberto Amaya, Edmundo Pérez,[24] the Ortega brothers[25] and Doris

---

18. Oscar Turcios was a Member of the FSLN National Directorate, assassinated by the National Guard at Nandaime on September 18th 1973.

19. Rigoberto Cruz ('Pablo Ubeda') was a member of the FSLN National Directorate. He directed FSLN political work among the mountain peasants between 1964-7, and was famous for his many disguises. He fell in combat at Pancasán in August 1967.

20. Carlos Reyna assisted Pablo Ubeda in his work among the peasants and fell at Pancasán in August 1967.

21. José Benito Escobar was a member of the FSLN National Directorate, assassinated in Estelí on June 15th 1978.

22. Enrique Lorente was killed in the La Ermita de Dolores *barrio* of León on April 13th 1970.

23. Francisco Moreno fell in combat at Pancasán in August 1967.

24. Roberto Amaya and Edmundo Pérez were captured by the National Guard in the Monseñor Lezcano *barrio* of Managua and then assassinated by the Security Forces (OSN) on November 4th 1967.

25. Camilo Ortega was sent by the FSLN to support the uprising of the Indians in the *barrio* of Monimbó, Masaya, where he was killed on February 26th 1978 in Las Sabogales, Masaya. After the triumph of the Revolution Daniel Ortega became President and Humberto Ortega Minister of Defence.

Tijerino.[26]

On November 25th, Carlos signs the FSLN communiqué *¡Sandino sí, Somoza no, Revolución sí, Farsa Electoral no!* *(Sandino yes, Somoza no, Revolution yes, Electoral Farce no!)* The other signatories are: Silvio Mayorga, Rigoberto Cruz, Oscar Turcios and Conchita Alday (pseudonym of Doris Tijerino). On December 7th he moves to Pancasán, in the centre of Nicaragua in the Matagalpa region, to reconnoitre a new guerrilla base.

1967

On January 27th, 60,000 take part in an electoral demonstration in Managua organised by the bourgeois opposition. 500 demonstrators are killed. The massacre destroys the credibility of the electoral farce as a means of overthrowing the dictatorship.

While developing guerrilla activities in Pancasán, Carlos has a confrontation with district 'justices', who denounce him to the National Guard. On August 27th at the Battle of Pancasán the National Guard decimate one guerrilla column, killing thirteen FSLN leaders. The FSLN abandons 'foquismo' – armed uprisings by small guerrilla bases *(focos)* – and expand their work among the peasantry and in towns. 1967-1974 becomes a period of 'silent accumulation of forces'.

1968

Carlos writes a letter to the parents of Francisco Moreno after his death at Pancasán, promising that FSLN will fight on and be worthy comrades of their fallen hero. On April 15th he issues a message to the Revolutionary Students.

1969

In February he departs secretly for Costa Rica to prepare future FSLN strategy. He is named FSLN Secretary General.

On July 15th FSLN National Directorate member Julio Buitrago is killed in a heroic shoot-out with the Guard, who surround his safe house in Managua. Doris Tijerino is taken prisoner.

On August 31st Carlos is captured in a safe house by the

---

26.   After the triumph of the Revolution, Doris Tijerino became head of the Sandinista police.

Costa Rican Criminal Investigation Department. On December 23rd the FSLN 'Juan Santamaría' Squad, led by Humberto Ortega and including Germán Pomares,[27] Rufo Marín,[28] Julián Roque, Fabián Rodríguez Mairena[29] and the Costa Rican Néstor Carvajal[30] mount an unsuccessful rescue operation. Rufo Marín and Humberto Ortega are seriously wounded and imprisoned.

1970

On January 15th the poet Leonel Rugama,[31] who had left the seminary where he was studying for the priesthood to join the FSLN, is killed in another shoot-out with the Guard in Managua, when his safe house is surrounded by troops, tanks and helicopters.

An international solidarity campaign, supported by Salvadoran poet Roque Dalton and French intellectuals Jean Paul Sartre and Simone de Beauvoir, demands the release of FSLN prisoners.

On October 21st Carlos Fonseca, Rufo Marín and Humberto Ortega are freed from prison by an FSLN action, led by Carlos Agüero,[32] involving a hijacked Costa Rican plane. They fly to Mexico and then on to Cuba. From there on November 7th, Carlos issues a *Message to the Nicaraguan People*.

1971

On March 27th he leaves Cuba, together with Carlos Agüero, Rufo Marín and others for Moscow and then on to Korea to receive military training. In June his essay 'Sandino, Guerrillero Proletario', written between December 1970 and February 1971, is published in the *Tricontinental* review. In September

---

27. Germán Pomares, known as 'El Danto' ('The Tapir'), Deputy Member of the FSLN National Directorate, fell in combat leading the attack on Jinotega on May 24th 1979, during the FSLN Final Offensive.
28. Rufo Marín was killed in Las Nubes, Jinotega on December 9th 1976.
29. Fabián Rodríguez Mairena was assassinated by the Security Forces (OSN) on October 3rd 1971, in Boaco.
30. Néstor Carvajal was accidentally killed in an FSLN training exercise.
31. There is a text and translation of some of Rugama's work, including his most famous poem, 'The Earth is a Satellite of the Moon', in *Poets of the Nicaraguan Revolution* (Katabasis 1993).
32. Carlos Agüero, Deputy Member of FSLN National Directorate, was killed in Lisawé, Zelaya, on April 7th 1977.

he returns to Cuba after a brief visit to China, and on September 15th he issues the *Mensaje del FSLN con Motivo del 150 Aniversario del Rompimiento del Yugo Colonial Español (FSLN Message on the 150th Anniversary of the Breaking of the Spanish Colonial Yoke)*. On October 1st the Cuban journal *Bohemia* publishes his work entitled 'El Frente Sandinista de Liberación Nacional'.

1972

On January 23rd the earthquake in Managua kills 10,000, injures a further 20,000 and leaves 300,000 homeless. The dictator embezzles the international relief aid.

On March 8th in Havana, Cuba, Carlos issues the document *Cronología Histórica de Nicaragua (Historical Chronology of Nicaragua)*. He writes the *Notas sobre la Carta-Testamento de Rigoberto López Pěrez (Notes on the Last Letter of Rigoberto López Pérez)*,[33] later published in *Casa de las Américas*.

1973

Carlos remains in Cuba and corresponds with the poet Ernesto Cardenal about his book *In Cuba*. Carlos also corresponds with Nicaraguans resident in the US. He has many discussions with FSLN militants.

In September the Nicaraguan National Guard announce his death at Nandaime, where on September 17th they had captured and murdered FSLN leaders Ricardo Morales and Oscar Turcios.

1974

Carlos writes his work on the poet Rubén Darío, later published in the journal *Casa de las Américas.* In September *Casa de las Américas* publishes his 'Augusto César Sandino ante sus Verdugos' ('Augusto César Sandino before his Executioners').

On December 27th Eduardo Contreras ('Comandante Marcos') leads an FSLN raid on the house of Somoza's Minister of Agriculture, 'Chema' Castillo, during a party for the dictator and US ambassador Turner B. Shelton. The guests are held to ransom until FSLN demands are met, which include the

---

33.   The text and translation of most of this letter are published in *Poets of the Nicaraguan Revolution* (Katabasis 1993).

release of political prisoners, among whom are Daniel Ortega and José Benito Escobar. This action ends the period of FSLN 'silent accumulation of forces'. The dictator declares a 'state of siege' and even fiercer repression ensues.

1975

Carlos is ratified as FSLN Secretary General. The FSLN splits into three tendencies. On November 3rd he issues the document *Síntesis de algunos Problemas Actuales (Summary of some Current Problems)* and secretly enters Nicaragua to try and sort them out. He is met by Carlos Agüero in León. He gives a short political and military training course to FSLN militants in a safe house in Las Piedrecitas, Managua.

1976

From March onwards, Carlos moves about inside Nicaragua, going from guerrilla camp to camp. He leaves León for Bocaycito in the Jinotega mountains, then moves on to the guerrilla camp at La Lana, Jinotega, accompanied by Claudia Chamorro,[34] Marlon Urbina and others. On the way they are detected by a group of district 'justices'.

They move on to the provisional camp at La Pioja and then towards the El Portal hills, Jinotega. Carlos moves on to the camp at San José de las Bayas, where at the end of July he is joined by Francisco Rivera ('Rubén') and Víctor Urbina ('Efraín') and in August, by Carlos Agüero.

In September this camp is discovered and bombed by the National Guard. The guerrillas retire deep within the mountain and during their retreat are encountered by the Guard. Carlos is wounded in the leg.

On October 8th 'from somewhere in the Segovian Mountains' he issues the document *Notas sobre la Montaña y algunos Otros Temas (Notes on the Mountain and Other Matters)*.

On November 7th, they continue their march towards Iyás in Zelaya. On November 8th in Boca de Piedra, in the district of Zinica, North Zelaya, Carlos Fonseca is killed in a shoot-out with the National Guard.

---

34.   Claudia Chamorro fell in combat at Las Bayas, Jinotega on January 9th 1977.